# EVOLVE

## STUDENT'S BOOK

with Digital Pack

Lindsay Clandfield, Ben Goldstein,
Ceri Jones, and Philip Kerr

# 2B

**CAMBRIDGE**
UNIVERSITY PRESS

Shaftesbury Road, Cambridge CB2 8EA, United Kingdom

One Liberty Plaza, 20th Floor, New York, NY 10006, USA

477 Williamstown Road, Port Melbourne, VIC 3207, Australia

314–321, 3rd Floor, Plot 3, Splendor Forum, Jasola District Centre, New Delhi – 110025, India

103 Penang Road, #05-06/07, Visioncrest Commercial, Singapore 238467

Cambridge University Press & Assessment is a department of the University of Cambridge.

It furthers the University's mission by disseminating knowledge in the pursuit of education, learning, and research at the highest international levels of excellence.

www.cambridge.org
Information on this title: www.cambridge.org/9781009231817

© Cambridge University Press & Assessment 2019, 2022

This publication is in copyright. Subject to statutory exception and to the provisions of relevant collective licensing agreements, no reproduction of any part may take place without the written permission of Cambridge University Press & Assessment.

First published with Digital Pack 2022

20  19  18  17  16  15  14  13

Printed in Poland by Opolgraf

*A catalogue record for this publication is available from the British Library*

ISBN 978-1-009-23170-1 Student's Book with eBook
ISBN 978-1-009-23179-4 Student's Book with Digital Pack
ISBN 978-1-009-23180-0 Student's Book with Digital Pack A
ISBN 978-1-009-23181-7 Student's Book with Digital Pack B
ISBN 978-1-108-40898-1 Workbook with Audio
ISBN 978-1-108-40863-9 Workbook with Audio A
ISBN 978-1-108-41192-9 Workbook with Audio B
ISBN 978-1-108-40516-4 Teacher's Edition with Test Generator
ISBN 978-1-108-41065-6 Presentation Plus
ISBN 978-1-108-41202-5 Class Audio CDs
ISBN 978-1-108-40788-5 Video Resource Book with DVD
ISBN 978-1-009-23152-7 Full Contact with Digital Pack

Additional resources for this publication at www.cambridge.org/evolve

Cambridge University Press & Assessment has no responsibility for the persistence or accuracy of URLs for external or third-party internet websites referred to in this publication, and does not guarantee that any content on such websites is, or will remain, accurate or appropriate. Information regarding prices, travel timetables, and other factual information given in this work is correct at the time of first printing but Cambridge University Press & Assessment does not guarantee the accuracy of such information thereafter.

# ACKNOWLEDGMENTS

The *Evolve* publishers would like to thank the following individuals and institutions who have contributed their time and insights into the development of the course:

José A. Alvarado Sotelo, **Summit English**, Mexico; Maria Araceli Hernández Tovar, **Instituto Tecnológico Superior de San Luis Potosí**, Capital, Mexico; Rosario Aste Rentería, **Instituto De Emprendedores USIL**, Peru; Kayla M. Briggs, **Hoseo University**, South Korea; Lenise Butler, **Laureate**, Mexico; Lílian Dantas; Aslı Derin Anaç, **İstanbul Bilgi University**, Turkey; Devon Derksen, **Myongji University**, South Korea; Roberta Freitas, **IBEU**, Rio de Janeiro, Brazil; Monica Frenzel, **Universidad Andrés Bello**, Chile; Gloria González Meza, **Instituto Politecnico Nacional, ESCA (University)**, Mexico; Elsa de loa Angeles Hernández Chérrez, **Centro de Idiomas, Universidad Técnica de Ambato**, Ecuador; José Manuel Cuin Jacuinde, **Coordinación de Lenguas Extranjeras del Instituto Tecnológico de Morelia**, Mexico; Thomas Christian Keller, **Universidad de las Américas**, Chile; Daniel Lowe, **Lowe English Services**, Panama; Antonio Machuca Montalvo, **Organización The Institute TITUELS, Veracruz**, Mexico; Daniel Martin, **CELLEP**, Brazil; Ivanova Monteros, **Universidad Tecnológica Equinoccial**, Ecuador; Verónica Nolivos Arellano, Language Coordinator, Quito, Ecuador; Daniel Nowatnick, **USA**; Claudia Piccoli Díaz, **Harmon Hall**, Mexico; Diego Ribeiro Santos, **Universidade Anhembri Morumbi**, São Paulo, Brazil; Maria del Socorro, **Universidad Autonoma del Estado de Mexico, Centro de enseñanza de lenguas (Toluca)**, Mexico; Heidi Vande Voort Nam, **Chongshin University**, South Korea; Isabela Villas Boas, **Casa Thomas Jefferson**, Brasilia, Brazil; Jason Williams, **Notre Dame Seishin University**, Japan; Matthew Wilson, **Miyagi University**, Japan.

To our student contributors, who have given us their ideas and their time, and who appear throughout this book:

Alessandra Avelar, Brazil; Noemi Irene Contreras Yañez, Mexico; Celeste María Erazo Flores, Honduras; Caio Henrique Gogenhan, Brazil; Lorena Martos Ahijado, Spain; Allison Raquel, Peru; Seung Geyoung Yang, South Korea.

And special thanks to Katy Simpson, teacher and writer at *myenglishvoice.com*; and Raquel Ribeiro dos Santos, EFL teacher, EdTech researcher, blogger, and lecturer.

**Authors' Acknowledgments:**

The authors would like to thank Daniel Isern for all his support in the early stages of the project. This book is dedicated to Groc.

**The authors and publishers acknowledge the following sources of copyright material and are grateful for the permissions granted. While every effort has been made, it has not always been possible to identify the sources of all the material used, or to trace all copyright holders. If any omissions are brought to our notice, we will be happy to include the appropriate acknowledgements on reprinting and in the next update to the digital edition, as applicable.**

**Text**:

Charles P. Gerba for the text on p. 98 from 'Hidden dangers in your office' by Dan Townend, *Express Newspapers* website, 12.06.2007. Copyright © Charles P. Gerba. Reproduced with kind permission; The Atlantic Media Co. for the text on p. 104 from 'A Musician Afraid of Sound' by Janet Horvath, 20.10.2015. Copyright © 2015 The Atlantic Media Co., as first published in the *Atlantic Magazine*. All rights reserved. Distributed by Tribune Content Agency.

**Photos**:

Key: B = Below, BG = Background, BL = Below Left, BR = Below Right, C = Centre, CL = Centre Left, CR = Centre Right, L = Left, R = Right, T = Top, TC = Top Centre, TL = Top Left, TR = Top Right.

All images are sourced from Getty Images.

p. xvi (photo 1): Klaus Vedfelt/DigitalVision; p. xvi (photo 2): Cultura RM Exclusive/dotdotred; p. 94 (woman jewelry): PeopleImages/DigitalVision;  p. 94 (advt baby): Bloomberg; p. 74, 84, 94, 106, 116, 126: Tom Merton/Caiaimage; p. 86 (necklace): Jose Luis Pelaez Inc/Blend Images/Getty Images Plus; p. 68 (drinking coffee), p. 121: Westend61; p. 90 (TR), p. 96: Hero Images; p. 66 (jar): Elizabeth Watt/Photolibrary; p. 66 (burger): LauriPatterson/E+; p. 66 (lettuce): Suzifoo/E+; p. 66 (chilli): Max2611/iStock/Getty Images Plus; p. 66 (strawberry): Samuel Jimenez/EyeEm; p. 66 (cereal): David Marsden/Photolibrary; p. 66 (yoghurt): Photoevent/E+; p. 66 (jam): Andy Crawford; p. 66 (corn): Diana Miller/Cultura; p. 66 (noodles): JTB Photo/ Universal Images Group Editorial; p. 66 (pasta): SvetlanaK/iStock/Getty Images Plus; p. 66 (salmon): Science Photo Library; p. 66 (avocado): Creative Crop/Photodisc; p. 66 (salt mill): Maximilian Stock Ltd./Photolibrary; p. 68 (egg): RyersonClark/iStock/Getty Images Plus; p. 68 (roast): StockFood; p. 68 (fish): yuriz/iStock/Getty Images Plus;

p. 68 (raw): ShyMan/E+; p. 68 (vegetables): Cristian Bortes/EyeEm; p. 68 (chilli): DianePeacock/E+; p. 68 (burgers grill): AVNphotolab/iStock/Getty Images Plus; p. 68 (eating lemon): Daniel Day/The Image Bank; p. 69 (que): Tetra Images; p. 70: BROOK PIFER/Taxi; p. 71: Eerik/E+; p. 73: Monty Rakusen/Cultura; p. 74 (meat): Jupiterimages/Stockbyte; p. 74 (cakes): DragonImages/iStock/Getty Images Plus; p. 74 (salad): fcafotodigital/iStock/Getty Images Plus; p. 75: Andrew Holt/The Image Bank; p. 76 (Deborah): Peathegee Inc/Blend Images; p. 76 (nico): heres2now.com/Moment; p. 76 (apartment): janeff/iStock/Getty Images Plus; p. 77 (opera house): Danita Delimont/Gallo Images; p. 77 (sugarloaf): Eduardo Garcia/Photographer's Choice; p. 77 (Golden Bridge): Jhoanna Reyes/EyeEm; p. 77 (Colisseum): Michael Duva/The Image Bank; p. 77 (Independence Monument): Jeremy Woodhouse/Photodisc; p. 77 (Mt. Fuji): I love Photo and Apple./Moment; p. 80: andresr/E+; p. 81: Roberto Machado Noa/LightRocket; p. 82 (man airport): Dana Neely/The Image Bank; p. 82 (woman airport): Hinterhaus Productions/Taxi; p. 83: kiszon pascal/Moment; p. 84 (theme park): Lou Jones/Lonely Planet Images; p. 84 (market): Linka A Odom/ Taxi; p. 84 (event): GDT/ The Image Bank; p. 85: DreamPictures/Vstock/Blend Images; p. 86 (boys tie): Steve Hix/Corbis; p. 86 (stylish): KristinaJovanovic/iStock/Getty Images Plus; p. 86 (socks): Laura Doss/Corbis/Getty Images Plus; p. 86 (bracelet): John Warburton-Lee/AWL Images; p. 86 (formals): Dave and Les Jacobs/Blend Images; p. 86 (20s man): Compassionate Eye Foundation/Hero Images/Taxi; p. 87: Peopleimages/E+; p. 88: Mark Hall/The Image Bank; p. 89: Jonathan Oswaldo Enriquez Huerta/EyeEm; p. 90 (TL): Nick David/Taxi; p. 91 (shirts): Gusto Images/Photodisc; p. 91 (shoes): Jan Stromme/The Image Bank; p. 91 (sunglasses): Koukichi Takahashi/EyeEm; p. 92 (photo a): UberImages/iStock/Getty Images Plus; p. 92 (photo b): Car Culture/Car Culture ® Collection; p. 92 (photo c): Christian Nittinger/EyeEm; p. 92 (photo d): Monashee Frantz/OJO Images; p. 94 (woman headphones): valentinrussanov/E+; p. 97: Harith Samarawickrama/Moment Open; p. 98 (chef): Jose Luis Pelaez Inc/ Blend Images; p. 98 (therapist): BSIP/Universal Images Group; p. 98 (mechanic): Jamie Garbutt/The Image Bank; p. 98 (architect): Letizia Le Fur/ONOKY; p. 98 (paramedic): LPETTET/E+; p. 98 (lawyer): RichLegg/E+; p. 98 (bacteria): Science Stills/Visuals Unlimited, Inc./Visuals Unlimited; p. 99: Stephanie Maze/Corbis Documentary; p. 101: Bill Varie/Corbis; p. 102: Brian Pieters/The Image Bank; p. 103 (band aid): wabeno/iStock/Getty Images Pluswabeno; p. 103 (plaster): Peter Dazeley/Photographer's Choice and Daniel Sambraus/EyeEm; p. 103 (blue plaster): Ccaetano/iStock/Getty Images Plus; p. 104: sot/Taxi; p. 106 (cops): LukaTDB/ iStock/Getty Images Plus; p. 106 (cooking): Jon Feingersh/Blend Images; p. 106 (renovation): GeorgePeters/iStock/Getty Images Plus; p. 106 (backpacker): Auscape/Universal Images Group; p. 107: milos-kreckovic/iStock/Getty Images Plus; p. 108 (Elena): Antonio_Diaz/iStock/Getty Images Plus; p. 108 (Maria): Blend Images - Frida Marquez/Brand X Pictures; p. 109: Anadolu Agency; p. 110 (male): michaelpuche/iStock/Getty Images Plus; p. 110 (young female): Sandeep Kapoor/EyeEm; p. 110 (old female): Shannon Fagan/Taxi; p. 111: AntonioGuillem/iStock/Getty Images Plus; p. 112 (broken phone): Ariel Skelley/DigitalVision; p. 112 (selfie): Betsie Van Der Meer/Taxi; p. 113: martinedoucet/E+; p. 116 (girl): JohnnyGreig/E+; p. 116 (food): mediaphotos/E+; p. 116 (tutorial): fstop123/E+; p. 117: Mint Images - Frans Lanting/Mint Images; p. 118 (wet): Tim Robberts/Taxi; p. 118 (cold): Attila Kocsis/EyeEm; p. 118 (hot): Karwai Tang/WireImage; p. 118 (stormy): john finney photography/Moment; p. 118 (extreme): Scott B Smith Photography/Photolibrary; p. 119: Christopher Wirth/EyeEm; p. 120 (quito): Reinier Snijders/EyeEm; p. 120 (tortoise): Antonio Salinas L./Moment; p. 122 (mobile): Bill Diodato/Corbis Documentary; p. 122 (nature): John Turp/Moment; p. 123 (Jason Hawkes/The Image Bank); p. 124 (gardening): Beau Lark/Corbis/VCG; p. 124 (flower): Laizah Mae Tano/EyeEm; p. 125: Kory Rogers/EyeEm; p. 126 (beach): Jeremy Koreski/All Canada Photos; p. 126 (lake): Aimin Tang/Photographer's Choice; p. 126 (rockies): TerenceLeezy/Moment; p. 149 (black man): verity jane smith/Blend Images; p. 149 (white girl): T. Fuchs/F1online; p. 149 (feet): baona/iStock/Getty Images Plus; p. 152 (photo a): fralo/iStock/Getty Images Plus; p. 152 (photo b): Gillian Henry/Moment; p. 152 (photo c): sara_winter/iStock/Getty Images Plus; p. 152 (photo d): Image Source/DigitalVision; p. 152 (photo e): Sam's photography/Moment.

The following images are sourced from other sources:

p. 72 (Impossible Burger): Courtesy of Impossible Foods Inc.

Clipart Courtesy of Noun Project Inc.

Front cover photography by Alija/E+/Getty Images.

Illustrations by: 290 Sean (KJA Artists) p. 100; Denis Cristo (Sylvie Poggio Artists Agency) p. 78; Ana Djordjevic (Astound US) p. 88; Lyn Dylan (Sylvie Poggio Artists Agency) p. 76; Martin Sanders (Beehive illustration) pp. 120, 152; Mark Watkinson (Illustration Web) p. 67.

Audio production by CityVox, New York

# EVOLVE

## SPEAKING MATTERS

EVOLVE is a six-level American English course for adults and young adults, taking students from beginner to advanced levels (CEFR A1 to C1).

Drawing on insights from language teaching experts and real students, EVOLVE is a general English course that gets students speaking with confidence.

This student-centered course covers all skills and focuses on the most effective and efficient ways to make progress in English.

## Confidence in teaching.
## Joy in learning.

**Better Learning WITH EVOLVE**

Better Learning is our simple approach where insights we've gained from research have helped shape content that drives results. Language evolves, and so does the way we learn. This course takes a flexible, student-centered approach to English language teaching.

EVOLVE
STUDENT'S BOOK
Lindsay Clandfield, Ben Goldstein, Ceri Jones, and Phillip Kerr
2

# Meet our student contributors ▶

Videos and ideas from real students feature throughout the Student's Book.

Our student contributors describe themselves in three words.

**ALESSANDRA AVELAR**

*Creative, positive, funny*
Faculdade ICESP, Águas
Claras, Brazil

**NOEMI IRENE
CONTRERAS YAÑEZ**

*Funny, intelligent, optimistic*
Universidad del Valle de
México, Mexico

**CELESTE MARÍA
ERAZO FLORES**

*Happy, special, friendly*
Unitec (Universidad Tecnologica
Centroamericana), Honduras

**CAIO HENRIQUE
GOGENHAN**

*Funny, lovely, smart*
Universidade Anhembi
Morumbi, Brazil

**ALLISON RAQUEL**

*Friendly, cheerful, intelligent*
Universidad Privada del
Norte, Peru

**SEUNG GEYOUNG YANG**

*Happy, creative*
Myongji University,
South Korea

**LORENA MARTOS AHIJADO**

*Cheerful, positive, kind*
Universidad Europea de
Madrid, Spain

# Student-generated content

EVOLVE is the first course of its kind to feature real student-generated content.
We spoke to over 2,000 students from all over the world about the topics they
would like to discuss in English and in what situations they would like to be able
to speak more confidently.

The ideas are included throughout the Student's Book and the students appear
in short videos responding to discussion questions.

## INSIGHT

Research shows that
achievable speaking role
models can be a powerful
motivator.

## CONTENT

Bite-sized videos feature
students talking about
topics in the Student's
Book.

## RESULT

Students are motivated
to speak and share their
ideas.

# "It's important to provide learners with interesting or stimulating topics."

Teacher, Mexico (Global Teacher Survey, 2017)

# Find it

## INSIGHT

Research with hundreds of teachers and students across the globe revealed a desire to expand the classroom and bring the real world in.

## CONTENT

*Find it* are smartphone activities that allow students to bring live content into the class and personalize the learning experience with research and group activities.

## RESULT

Students engage in the lesson because it is meaningful to them.

# Designed for success

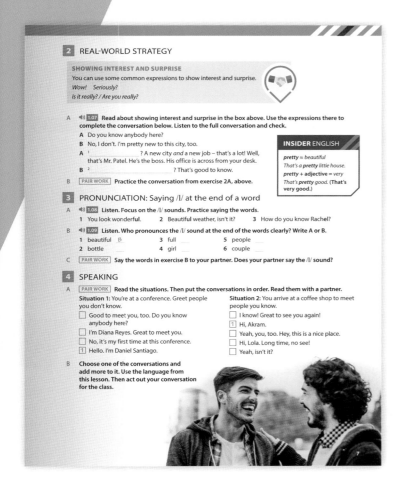

## Pronunciation

### INSIGHT

Research shows that only certain aspects of pronunciation actually affect comprehensibility and inhibit communication.

### CONTENT

EVOLVE focuses on the aspects of pronunciation that most affect communication.

### RESULT

Students understand more when listening and can be clearly understood when they speak.

## Insider English

### INSIGHT

Even in a short exchange, idiomatic language can inhibit understanding.

### CONTENT

*Insider English* focuses on the informal language and colloquial expressions frequently found in everyday situations.

### RESULT

Students are confident in the real world.

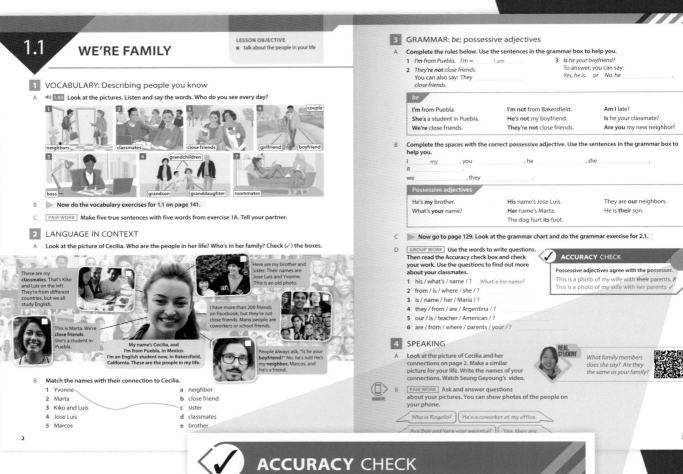

# Accuracy check

## INSIGHT

Some common errors can become fossilized if not addressed early on in the learning process.

## CONTENT

*Accuracy check* highlights common learner errors (based on unique research into the Cambridge Learner Corpus) and can be used for self-editing.

## RESULT

Students avoid common errors in their written and spoken English.

"The presentation is very clear and there are plenty of opportunities for student practice and production."

Jason Williams, Teacher, Notre Dame Seishin University, Japan

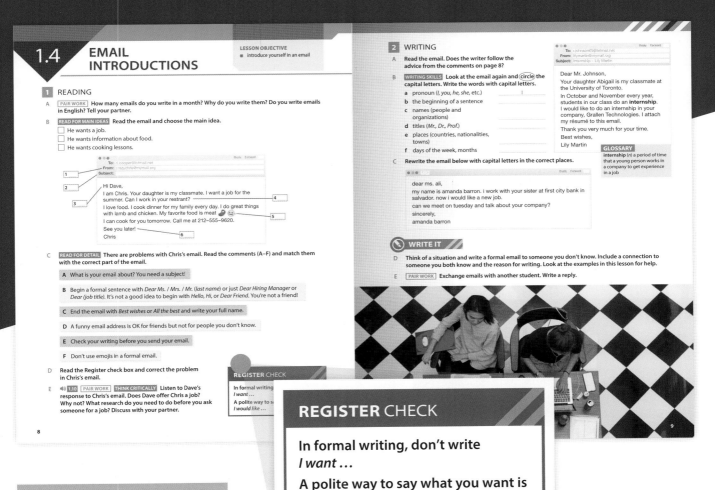

## 1.4 EMAIL INTRODUCTIONS

**LESSON OBJECTIVE**
■ introduce yourself in an email

### 1 READING

A [PAIR WORK] How many emails do you write in a month? Why do you write them? Do you write emails in English? Tell your partner.

B [READ FOR MAIN IDEAS] Read the email and choose the main idea.
- ☐ He wants a job.
- ☐ He wants information about food.
- ☐ He wants cooking lessons.

To: d.cooper@hotmail.net
From: crazychris@mymail.org
Subject:

Hi Dave,
I am Chris. Your daughter is my classmate. I want a job for the summer. Can I work in your restrant?
I love food. I cook dinner for my family every day. I do great things with lamb and chicken. My favorite food is meat 🍖 🍗
I can cook for you tomorrow. Call me at 212–555–9620.
See you later!
Chris

1  2  3  4  5  6

C [READ FOR DETAIL] There are problems with Chris's email. Read the comments (A–F) and match them with the correct part of the email.

A What is your email about? You need a subject!

B Begin a formal sentence with *Dear Ms. / Mrs. / Mr.* (last name) or just *Dear Hiring Manager* or *Dear (job title)*. It's not a good idea to begin with *Hello, Hi,* or *Dear Friend*. You're not a friend!

C End the email with *Best wishes* or *All the best* and write your full name.

D A funny email address is OK for friends but not for people you don't know.

E Check your writing before you send your email.

F Don't use emojis in a formal email.

D Read the Register check box and correct the problem in Chris's email.

E 🔊 1-10 [PAIR WORK] [THINK CRITICALLY] Listen to Dave's response to Chris's email. Does Dave offer Chris a job? Why not? What research do you need to do before you ask someone for a job? Discuss with your partner.

**REGISTER** CHECK
In formal writing
*I want* …
A polite way to s…
*I would like* …

8

### 2 WRITING

A Read the email. Does the writer follow the advice from the comments on page 8?

B [WRITING SKILLS] Look at the email again and circle the capital letters. Write the words with capital letters.
- a pronoun (*I, you, he, she,* etc.) ____
- b the beginning of a sentence ____
- c names (people and organizations) ____
- d titles (*Mr., Dr., Prof.*) ____
- e places (countries, nationalities, towns) ____
- f days of the week, months ____

To: r.johnson65@hotmail.net
From: lilymartin@mymail.org
Subject: Internship – Lily Martin

Dear Mr. Johnson,
Your daughter Abigail is my classmate at the University of Toronto.
In October and November every year, students in our class do an **internship**. I would like to do an internship in your company, Grallen Technologies. I attach my résumé to this email.
Thank you very much for your time.
Best wishes,
Lily Martin

**GLOSSARY**
**internship** (*n*) a period of time that a young person works in a company to get experience in a job

C Rewrite the email below with capital letters in the correct places.

dear ms. ali,
my name is amanda barron. i work with your sister at first city bank in salvador. now i would like a new job.
can we meet on tuesday and talk about your company?
sincerely,
amanda barron

### ✏ WRITE IT

D Think of a situation and write a formal email to someone you don't know. Include a connection to someone you both know and the reason for writing. Look at the examples in this lesson for help.

E [PAIR WORK] Exchange emails with another student. Write a reply.

9

## Register check

**REGISTER** CHECK

In formal writing, don't write
*I want* …

A polite way to say what you want is
*I would like* …

### INSIGHT
Teachers report that their students often struggle to master the differences between written and spoken English.

### CONTENT
*Register check* draws on research into the Cambridge English Corpus and highlights potential problem areas for learners.

### RESULT
Students transition confidently between written and spoken English and recognize different levels of formality as well as when to use them appropriately.

ix

# You spoke. We listened.

Students told us that speaking is the most important skill for them to master, while teachers told us that finding speaking activities which engage their students and work in the classroom can be challenging.

That's why EVOLVE has a whole lesson dedicated to speaking: Lesson 5, *Time to speak*.

## Time to speak

### INSIGHT

Speaking ability is how students most commonly measure their own progress, but is also the area where they feel most insecure. To be able to fully exploit speaking opportunities in the classroom, students need a safe speaking environment where they can feel confident, supported, and able to experiment with language.

### CONTENT

*Time to Speak* is a unique lesson dedicated to developing speaking skills and is based around immersive tasks which involve information sharing and decision making.

### RESULT

*Time to speak* lessons create a buzz in the classroom where speaking can really thrive, evolve, and take off, resulting in more confident speakers of English.

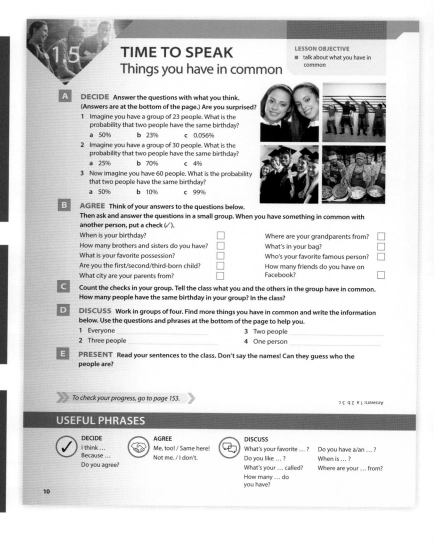

Experience Better Learning with EVOLVE: a course that helps both teachers and students on every step of the language learning journey.

Speaking matters. Find out more about creating safe speaking environments in the classroom.

# EVOLVE unit structure

## Unit opening page

Each unit opening page activates prior knowledge and vocabulary and immediately gets students speaking.

## Lessons 1 and 2

These lessons present and practice the unit vocabulary and grammar in context, helping students discover language rules for themselves. Students then have the opportunity to use this language in well-scaffolded, personalized speaking tasks.

## Lesson 3

This lesson is built around a functional language dialogue that models and contextualizes useful fixed expressions for managing a particular situation. This is a real world strategy to help students handle unexpected conversational turns.

## Lesson 4

This is a combined skills lesson based around an engaging reading or listening text. Each lesson asks students to think critically and ends with a practical writing task.

## Lesson 5

*Time to speak* is an entire lesson dedicated to developing speaking skills. Students work on collaborative, immersive tasks which involve information sharing and decision making.

# CONTENTS

| | Learning objectives | Grammar | Vocabulary | Pronunciation |
|---|---|---|---|---|
| **Unit 7**<br>Eat, drink, be happy | ■ Talk about your favorite comfort food<br>■ Design a food truck<br>■ Explain what you want in a restaurant<br>■ Write a comment about an online article<br>■ Plan a party | ■ Quantifiers<br>■ Verb patterns | ■ Naming food<br>■ Describing food | ■ /dʒ/ and /g/ sounds |
| **Unit 8**<br>Trips | ■ Discuss what to do in your town<br>■ Talk about a trip you went on<br>■ Give advice and make suggestions<br>■ Write advice on living in another country<br>■ Plan a short trip | ■ *if* and *when*<br>■ Giving reasons using *to* and *for* | ■ Traveling<br>■ Transportation | ■ Long and short vowel sounds<br>■ Listening for intonation |
| **Unit 9**<br>Looking good | ■ Compare stores and what they sell<br>■ Talk about people in photos<br>■ Ask for and give opinions<br>■ Write a paragraph describing a photo<br>■ Create and present an ad | ■ Comparative adjectives<br>■ Superlative adjectives | ■ Accessories<br>■ Appearance | ■ /ɜ/ vowel sound |
| **Review 3 (Review of Units 7–9)** | | | | |
| **Unit 10**<br>Risky business | ■ Talk about how to avoid danger at work<br>■ Make predictions about your future<br>■ Describe a medical problem and ask for help<br>■ Write an email to your future self<br>■ Plan a reality TV show | ■ *have to*<br>■ Making predictions | ■ Jobs<br>■ Health problems | ■ Final consonant sounds |
| **Unit 11**<br>Me, online | ■ Talk about what you've done and what you've never done<br>■ Talk about what you've done, and when<br>■ Make and respond to requests<br>■ Write comments about an infographic<br>■ Create a video or vlog | ■ Present perfect for experience<br>■ Present perfect and simple past | ■ Verb-noun internet phrases<br>■ Social media verbs | ■ Final /m/ and /n/ sounds |
| **Unit 12**<br>Outdoors | ■ Talk about the weather<br>■ Describe places, people, and things<br>■ Ask for and give directions<br>■ Write simple instructions<br>■ Create a tourism campaign for your country | ■ *be like*<br>■ Relative pronouns: *who, which, that* | ■ Weather<br>■ Landscapes and cityscapes | ■ /w/ at the beginning of a word<br>■ Listening for *t* when it sounds like d |
| **Review 4 (Review of Units 10–12)** | | | | |

**Grammar charts and practice, pages 135–140    Vocabulary exercises, pages 147–152**

| Functional language | Listening | Reading | Writing | Speaking |
|---|---|---|---|---|
| ■ Order food; take an order; ask questions about food; ask for the check<br>**Real-world strategy**<br>■ *I mean* | | **Foods**<br>■ An article about the Impossible Burger | **Comments on Impossible Foods**<br>■ A comment on an article<br>■ *I (don't) think; If you ask me; For me* | ■ Talk about special meals<br>■ Talk about your favorite comfort food<br>■ Talk about a food truck<br>■ Order food from a menu<br>**Time to speak**<br>■ Talk about the perfect party |
| ■ Give advice and make suggestions; respond to advice and suggestions<br>**Real-world strategy**<br>■ Echo questions | **Leaving home**<br>■ A radio show about living in another country | | **Listeners' comments**<br>■ A comment on advice from listeners<br>■ Phrases to respond to advice | ■ Talk about a good vacation<br>■ Talk about your town<br>■ Talk about a long trip you took<br>■ Give advice to a visitor in your town<br>**Time to speak**<br>■ Talk about planning a trip |
| ■ Ask for an opinion; give a positive opinion; give a negative or neutral opinion<br>**Real-world strategy**<br>■ *I guess* | | **Image is everything**<br>■ An article about advertising | **Advertising contest**<br>■ An email submission to a contest<br>■ Punctuation: periods, capital letters, and commas | ■ Talk about appearance<br>■ Compare clothes stores<br>■ Talk about your best photos<br>■ Give your opinion of clothes<br>**Time to speak**<br>■ Talk about making an ad |
| ■ Offer help; ask for information about the problem; ask someone for help<br>**Real-world strategy**<br>■ *It's like / It feels like* | | **Face your fears**<br>■ An article about a personal experience | **An email to myself**<br>■ An email giving advice<br>■ *anyway, by the way* | ■ Talk about things you're afraid of<br>■ Talk about dangers at work or study<br>■ Predict future events<br>■ Explain a medical problem<br>**Time to speak**<br>■ Talk about reality TV |
| ■ Make requests; respond to requests; ask for permission; refusing<br>**Real-world strategy**<br>■ Remember words | | **Selfies**<br>■ An infographic | **Positive and negative comments**<br>■ A short comment on selfies<br>■ Saying something positive or negative | ■ Talk about screens<br>■ Ask and answer questions about experiences<br>■ Ask and answer questions about online habits<br>■ Make requests in specific situations<br>**Time to speak**<br>■ Talk about online videos |
| ■ Ask for directions; give directions<br>**Real-world strategy**<br>■ Correct yourself | **Guerrilla gardening**<br>■ An interview with a guerrilla gardener | | **How to …**<br>■ A list of instructions on how to do something<br>■ *first, then, next, now, finally* | ■ Talk about hot and cold weather<br>■ Talk about weather in different cities in the world<br>■ Talk about people, objects, and places<br>■ Ask for directions, check you understand<br>**Time to speak**<br>■ Talk about advertising your country |

# CLASSROOM LANGUAGE

🔊 **1.02** **Asking for help**

How do you say that in English?

What does _____ mean?

How do you spell _____ ?

How do you pronounce this word?

Sorry, can you repeat that, please?

Sorry, I don't understand.

**Working in pairs and groups**

Who wants to start?

Who wants to go first?

Whose turn is it?

It's my turn.

It's your turn.

OK. What do you have for number 1?

Let's compare answers.

# EAT, DRINK, BE HAPPY

**7**

**UNIT OBJECTIVES**

- talk about your favorite comfort food
- design a food truck
- explain what you want in a restaurant
- write a comment about an online article
- plan a party

## START SPEAKING

A   Look at the picture. Who are these people? Why are they all eating together? Do you have big meals like this? When?

B   In general, do you prefer eating alone or with other people? Who do you usually eat with at different meals? What do you talk about when you're eating?

C   What makes a meal special: Is it the food, the people, or something else? Explain your answer. For ideas, watch Seung Geyoung's video.

**REAL STUDENT**

*Do you agree with Seung Geyoung?*

# COMFORT FOOD

## 1 VOCABULARY: Naming food

A 🔊 **2.02** **Look at the pictures. Which do you like? With a partner, match the food items to the words in the box. Listen and check, and then say the words.**

| | |
|---|---|
| avocado ___ | onion ___ |
| burger ___ | pasta ___ |
| cereal ___ | peanut butter _1_ |
| chili / chili pepper ___ | pepper ___ |
| corn ___ | salmon ___ |
| jam ___ | salt ___ |
| lettuce ___ | strawberry ___ |
| noodles ___ | yogurt ___ |

B **Which food items are sweet, and which are usually not sweet? Make two lists.**

C ▶ **Now do the vocabulary exercises for 7.1 on page 147.**

## 2 LANGUAGE IN CONTEXT

A **What is "comfort food"? Read the blog post and find out. How many different types of chicken soup does the writer describe?**

# A TASTE OF HOME

Everyone has their own idea of comfort food — that special dish you eat anytime you feel sad or worried.

For me, there's only one comfort food: my mom's chicken soup. Did you know that chicken soup is probably the world's favorite comfort food? It makes you feel happy, and it's quick to make – perfect when there's not much time to cook.

The classic recipe includes chicken and a little **onion**, but there are many other ways to cook it. Colombian *ajiaco* has a lot of **corn** and potatoes, in India it comes with an egg, and the Chinese serve it with **noodles** and sometimes a few **chilies**. In Korea they usually eat *samgyetang* in the summer, served with some rice.

Comfort food is very personal. It can be a full meal, a dessert, or just a snack. Tell us about *your* favorite comfort food.

B **PAIR WORK** **Find these words in the blog: *dessert, dish, meal, snack*. Think of an example of each one.**

FIND IT

C **PAIR WORK** **What's a famous soup in your country? Where and when do people usually eat it? You can go online to find a recipe. For ideas, watch Alessandra's video.**

**REAL STUDENT**

*Would you like to try Alessandra's dish?*

## 3 GRAMMAR: Quantifiers

A Complete the rules. Use the pictures in the grammar box to help you. Which words can you use to talk about a large amount, a small amount, and an amount that is not large or small?

1 Count nouns (e.g., *strawberry, avocado*) can be **only singular** / **only plural** / **singular or plural**.

2 Use *a* or _____ with singular count nouns.

**Quantifiers**

**Count nouns**
*How many chilies?*

a lot of chilies          **some** chilies

**a few** / **not many** chilies          **too many** chilies

**Non-count nouns**
*How much rice?*

**a lot of** rice          **some** rice

**a little** / **not much** rice          **too much** rice

---

**!** Some nouns can be count *and* non-count.
You can count chili peppers (*too many chilies*) but not the small pieces we use for cooking (*too much chili*).
Think about *chicken*. When is it count, and when is it non-count?

---

B ▶ Now go to page 135. Look at the grammar chart and do the grammar exercise for 7.1.

C Complete the questions with *much* or *many*. Then check your accuracy. Ask your partner the questions.

1 How ___*many*___ cups of coffee do you drink every day?
2 How _____ cookies do you eat in a week?
3 How _____ yogurt do you eat at breakfast?
4 How _____ meat or fish do you eat each week?

✓ **ACCURACY** CHECK

Use *many* with plural count nouns.

There aren't ~~much~~ chilies in this dish. ✗
There aren't many chilies in this dish. ✓

## 4 SPEAKING

A **PAIR WORK** Tell your partner about your favorite comfort food.

 My favorite comfort food is … It's my favorite food because … I like to eat it with some / a lot of / a little …

B **GROUP WORK** Ask other students about their favorite comfort food. Tell the class.

A lot of people like snacks and sweet food. Manuel's favorite comfort food is rice with milk and sugar.

# EAT IN THE STREET

## 1 VOCABULARY: Describing food

A 🔊 **2.03** Listen and say the words. Now match the words to the pictures.

| bitter | boiled | delicious | fresh | fried | grilled | raw | roasted | sour | spicy |

1 boiled
2
3
4
5
6
7
8
9
10

B Put the words in exercise 1A into two groups: (a) how to serve food and (b) how food tastes. One word can go in both groups. Which word?

C ▶ Now do the vocabulary exercises for 7.2 on page 147.

## 2 LANGUAGE IN CONTEXT

A PAIR WORK Look at the picture of a food truck. What kinds of food can you get from food trucks?

B 🔊 **2.04** Listen to a live radio show from the Food Truck Awards. What food is Clara cooking today? Why does the customer like food trucks?

🔊 **2.04 Audio script**

| | |
|---|---|
| **Host** | Hi! I'm at the Food Truck Awards with one of this year's winners, Clara Montero. What are you making today, Clara? |
| **Clara** | Fish tacos! They're usually **fried**, but today the fish is **raw**. Try one! It has this great **spicy** sauce. |
| **Host** | Mm! Wow, hot! But really good. Thanks, Clara. Now, I'm sure this next truck is good because there's a long line. Hi! What are you waiting here for? |
| **Customer** | Their amazing **grilled** burgers! I usually can't stand waiting in line, but I don't mind waiting here. |
| **Host** | Yeah? Better than a restaurant? |
| **Customer** | Definitely! I prefer to eat at food trucks. They're really cool – they're cheap, you can eat outside, and the food is always **delicious**. I always want to try new food. You need to try their fries. They're amazing! |
| **Host** | Great idea, thanks. Enjoy! |

**INSIDER** ENGLISH

*hot = spicy*

C PAIR WORK Are there many food trucks in your town? What's your favorite dish?

## 3 GRAMMAR: Verb patterns

**A** (Circle) the correct options to complete the rules. Use the sentences in the grammar box to help you.

1 The verb that follows verbs like *can't stand* and *don't mind* is **verb + -ing / to + verb**.

2 The verb that follows verbs like *want* and *need* is **verb + -ing / to + verb**.

> **Verb patterns**
>
> I usually **can't stand waiting** in line.    I always **want to try** new food.
> I **don't mind waiting** here.                You **need to try** their fries.

**B** ▶ Now go to page 135. Look at the grammar chart and do the grammar exercise for 7.2.

**C** [PAIR WORK] Choose verbs from each box and make true sentences about yourself. Tell your partner.

| can't stand | don't mind | enjoy | forget | hate |
|---|---|---|---|---|
| like | love | prefer | want | would like |

| buy | cook | eat | go out | make | shop | take |
|---|---|---|---|---|---|---|

> **!** Some verbs (*love, prefer, like, hate*) take both forms. The meaning doesn't change.
> *I like to cook.* ✓
> *I like cooking.* ✓
> *I prefer to eat out.* ✓
> *I prefer eating out.* ✓

💬 I can't stand cooking breakfast food. It's so boring!

## 4 SPEAKING

**A** [GROUP WORK] **You are going to design your own food truck. Think about:**

- the name and look of your food truck
- what's on the menu and how it's cooked
- the prices of your food and any special deals
- who your customers are (for example, vegetarians, students)

💬 Our food truck is called Crepe Crazy. We're going to sell all types of delicious crepes like peanut butter, cheese and onion, and strawberry. Everyone enjoys eating crepes but hates to make them at home. Our prices . . . .

**B** Tell the class about your food truck. Which group's food truck is the best?

# 7.3 I'LL HAVE THE CHICKEN

**LESSON OBJECTIVE**
■ explain what you want in a restaurant

## 1 FUNCTIONAL LANGUAGE

A  🔊 **2.05** **Read and listen to the conversations. What does the woman order in conversation 1? Why? In conversation 2, what's the problem with her order? In conversation 3, what does she ask for?**

🔊 **2.05 Audio script**

**1** **A** Hi, **are you ready to order?**
   **B** **What do you recommend?**
   **A** The seafood's great here.
   **B** But I'm allergic to seafood.
   **A** Well, the grilled salmon is fantastic.
   **B** I mean, I'm allergic to all seafood.
   **A** Oh, OK. Well, the chicken is very good.
   **B** **What does it come with?**
   **A** It comes with French fries and a salad.
   **B** **What kind of dressing** does it come with?
   **A** Oil and vinegar.
   **B** Perfect. **I'll have the** chicken, please.

**2** **B** Excuse me – you gave me the salmon, but I ordered grilled chicken.
   **A** I'm so sorry. I'll bring you the correct dish right away.
   **B** Thank you.

**3** **A** **Was everything OK for you today?**
   **B** It was all really good, thank you.
   **A** **Can I get you** a dessert?
   **B** Not today, thanks. **Can I have the check?**
   **A** Sure. Coming right up.

B  **Complete the chart with expressions in bold from the conversations above.**

| Ordering food | | Taking an order | |
|---|---|---|---|
| I'll ¹_____ the (chicken), please. | | Are you ready ⁵_____ _____ ? | |
| | | Can I ⁶_____ _____ (a dessert)? | |
| **Asking questions about food** | | **Checking with the customer** | |
| What do you ²_____ ? | | ⁷_____ _____ OK for you today? | |
| What does it ³_____ _____ ? | | **Asking for the check** | |
| | | Can I ⁸_____ the check? | |
| What ⁴_____ (dressing) does it come with? | | | |

C  🔊 **2.06** PAIR WORK (Circle) **the correct word to complete the expressions. Listen and check. Then practice the conversations with a partner. Change the food each time.**

**1** **A** What does the steak *go / come* with?
   **B** Salad or fries.
**2** **A** *How / What* was the chicken?
   **B** Great, thanks. Can I *have / make* the check, please?

## 2 REAL-WORLD STRATEGY

A 🔊 2.07 Listen to another conversation in the restaurant. What does the customer ask about the pasta?

B 🔊 2.07 Listen again. Why does the customer say, *I mean … ?*

> **I MEAN**
>
> When you need to be clear about an order or instruction, or if you think someone doesn't really understand what you want, use *I mean* to give more detail.
>
> *Is there any meat in the pasta? I'm a vegetarian.*
> *There's a little meat in the sauce, but not much.*
> *I mean, I don't eat any meat.*

C PAIR WORK Read the information about *I mean* in the box above. Practice the example conversation with a partner.

D ▶ PAIR WORK Student A: Go to page 158. Student B: Go to page 160. Follow the instructions.

## 3 PRONUNCIATION: Saying /dʒ/ and /g/ sounds

A 🔊 2.08 Listen to the words. Focus on the sound of the letters in **bold**. Practice saying them.

/dʒ/ **j**et    /g/ **g**et

B 🔊 2.09 Look at the conversation. Do the **bold** words have the /dʒ/ sound or the /g/ sound? Listen and check. Then practice the conversation with a partner.

A Can I **g**et you some **j**uice? We have **g**reat apple **j**uice.

B No, thanks. I'm aller**g**ic to apple **j**uice.

A **G**ot it. Just some water, then?

## 4 SPEAKING

A PAIR WORK Put the conversation in order. Then practice with a partner.

5 Sounds good. I'll have the pasta.

☐ It's a cream and mushroom sauce.

☐ What do you recommend? The pasta or the beef?

☐ What kind of sauce does it have?

☐ The pasta is delicious today.

B PAIR WORK Choose one of the situations and have a conversation with your partner.

- The server brings the wrong dish to a customer.
- The server doesn't understand the customer's question.
- The customer is allergic to peanuts.

# IMPOSSIBLE FOODS

## 1 READING

A **PREDICT** Look at the picture in the article. Why do you think this is called the Impossible Burger?

B Read the article. Were you right? Read the article again and write the headings in the correct places.

1 In a restaurant near you

2 Meat from plants

3 Good for the future

4 The secret ingredient

C **PAIR WORK** **THINK CRITICALLY** Read the article again. Are Impossible Burgers the best thing to happen to food in years? Discuss the positives and negatives of green food with your partner.

# The new and wonderful world of Impossible Foods

**A** _____

Impossible Foods is a company in Silicon Valley, California. They make burgers and other delicious meat and dairy products. There's something very unusual about their food: Their meat and dairy don't come from animals, but from plants. Yes, plants! I didn't believe it at first, but it's true. Thanks to Impossible Foods, you can eat a delicious burger that looks like meat and tastes like meat but is made with only plants.

**B** _____

How does the Impossible Burger look and taste so real? The secret is something called heme. It's an ingredient that exists in both plants and animals. Heme gives raw beef its red color and meat flavor. Impossible Foods uses the heme found in plants, not animals, to make the Impossible Burger. It's healthy, and the plant ingredients don't hurt the environment. Clever, isn't it?

**C** _____

So, why is Impossible Foods doing this? Well, animal farming uses about 50% of the Earth's land and 25% of the Earth's water. That's a very expensive way to produce food. So, it seems to me that the Impossible Burger is a great example of a food of the future – good for the planet and good for your health. Soon it'll be cheap to eat, too!

**D** _____

Maybe you think all of this is science fiction, but it's not. Twenty restaurants in the U.S. now sell the Impossible Burger. Soon these delicious burgers will be everywhere. In my opinion, it's the best thing to happen to food in years!

**GLOSSARY**

**dairy** (*adj*) milk products, or food made from milk

## 2 WRITING

**A** Look at the comments posted about the article. Who is positive, and who is negative about Impossible Foods?

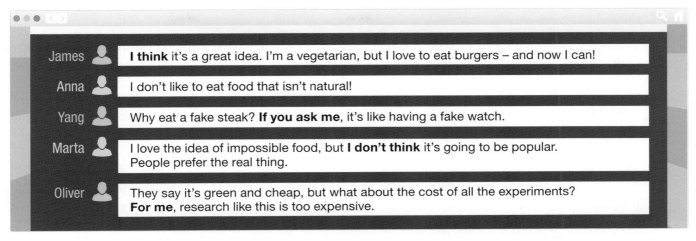

James **I think** it's a great idea. I'm a vegetarian, but I love to eat burgers – and now I can!

Anna I don't like to eat food that isn't natural!

Yang Why eat a fake steak? **If you ask me**, it's like having a fake watch.

Marta I love the idea of impossible food, but **I don't think** it's going to be popular. People prefer the real thing.

Oliver They say it's green and cheap, but what about the cost of all the experiments? **For me**, research like this is too expensive.

**B** PAIR WORK Look at the comments again. Which comments do you agree and disagree with? Why?

**C** WRITING SKILLS Look at the words in **bold** in the comments. Do we use these expressions to say something is true or to give an opinion?

**D** Read the Register check box. Then rewrite these sentences with a different expression than *I think*.

1 I think Impossible Foods is a great company!

2 I think it's a crazy idea. I don't like food made by scientists.

3 I think it's good for the planet!

### REGISTER CHECK

Here are some ways to give an opinion:

*I think … If you ask me … For me …*

For formal writing, like essays, use a more formal expression:

*From my point of view …*
*It seems to me that …*

## WRITE IT

**E** Do you think foods like the impossible burger are a good idea? Write a comment about it to post on the website.

# TIME TO SPEAK
## The perfect party

FIND IT

**A** When do you celebrate? Who do you celebrate with? Do you have parties to celebrate special occasions? What food do people usually eat at celebrations in your country? You can go online to find examples. What's your favorite party food? Why?

**B** PREPARE Imagine you and your partner are party organizers. You are going to organize a party for another pair, your "clients." Ask the other pair these questions to help you decide the type of party you're going to organize.

## Your perfect party

### Occasion
What are you celebrating?

### People
Would you like to invite a lot of people or a few close friends?

Would you like to invite your family?

### Place
Do you want to celebrate at home, in a restaurant, or in another place?

Would you like to be inside or outside?

### Food
Do you and your friends like to eat spicy food?

Do you prefer to eat fried food or grilled food?

Do you need to think about special diets?

### Surprise
Do you like surprises?

**C** DECIDE Use your clients' answers in exercise B to plan your party. Use the phrases at the bottom of the page to help you.

**D** DISCUSS Tell your clients about the party you're planning for them. Then listen to their plans for your party. Say two things you like about the party and two things you would like to change.

**E** PRESENT Present your parties to the class. Which one sounds fun? Which menu is your favorite? Why?

>> *To check your progress, go to page 155.* >>

# USEFUL PHRASES

**PREPARE**
I'd like that. / I wouldn't like that.
I'd prefer …
My brother is a vegetarian/vegan.
My friend is allergic to nuts/fish/milk, etc.

**DECIDE**
Let's invite …
The party will take place in …
We'll have … on the menu.

**DISCUSS**
I really like that idea.
I'd love to come to your party!
It sounds like fun!
We think you're going to love this.
What do you think of … ?

**8**

- discuss what to do in your town
- talk about a trip you went on
- give advice and make suggestions
- write advice on living in another country
- plan a short trip

## START SPEAKING

A **Look at the picture. What adjectives can you use to describe it? Would you like to go there?**

B **Which things are important to you when you're on vacation? Check (✓) your top <u>three</u> choices.**

- ☐ a beautiful place
- ☐ good food
- ☐ doing nothing
- ☐ doing lots of things
- ☐ meeting new people
- ☐ traveling with friends

REAL STUDENT

*Does Celeste's vacation sound fun to you?*

C **Where did you go on your last vacation? What did you do? Did you have fun? For ideas, watch Celeste's video.**

## 1 VOCABULARY: Traveling

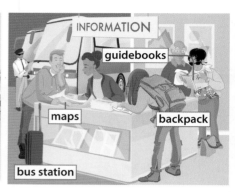

A 🔊 **2.10** **Look at the pictures. Listen and say the words in the pictures. Which words are (a) people, (b) places, (c) things you bring on vacation, or (d) types of transportation?**

> **!** *luggage* = carry-on bags, suitcases, and large backpacks.

B ▶ **Now do the vocabulary exercises for 8.1 on page 148.**

C **PAIR WORK** **Answer the questions with a partner.**

1 How much do you take with you for a weekend away, one suitcase, a backpack? What about for a long vacation?

2 Do many tourists come to your town? Where do you usually see them?

3 When you visit a new city, do you prefer to use a tourist map or your phone? Do you usually buy a guidebook? Why or why not?

## 2 LANGUAGE IN CONTEXT

A **Deborah rented a room in her Vancouver home to Nico for five days. Read their reviews of the experience. Did Deborah and Nico enjoy the activities they did together? Why or why not?**

# Home Here and There

**Review your guest**
Nico was a great guest. Most days he explored the city on his own. I gave him a **map** and some **guidebooks**. On the weekend, I was his **tour guide**. I'm always happy to help if my guests want a local guide. We visited lots of interesting landmarks together. When I'm with my guests, I always have a good time. It's like being a **tourist** in my own town!

**Review your stay**

If you stay in someone's home, you get a good idea of life there. I rented a room in Deborah's apartment. It's right in the heart of downtown. Perfect! Deborah was a great host. On the weekend, I really wanted to go hiking in the mountains, but she took me to a classical music concert instead. Not really my thing. Most days, I borrowed a guidebook from her and explored on my own, so it was OK. Vancouver is a great city!

B **PAIR WORK** (Circle) the words in the reviews on page 76 that mean the following. Add them to your lists in exercise 1A.

1 a person who is staying in your home
2 to go around a place you don't know
3 the famous and important places in a town or city
4 a person who welcomes a guest into his or her home

C **PAIR WORK** Would you like to be a host and have a guest in your home for money? Would you like to rent a room in someone's home when you travel? Why or why not?

## 3 GRAMMAR: *if* and *when*

A (Circle) the correct options to complete the rules. Use the sentences in the grammar box to help you.

1 Use *if* / *when* and the simple present to say that something happens only after another thing happens first.

2 Use *if* / *when* and the simple present to say that something happens at almost the same time as another thing happens.

> **if and when**
>
> I'm always happy to help **if** my guests want a local guide.
>
> **When** I'm with my guests, I always have a good time.
>
> **If** you stay in someone's home, you get a good idea of life there.

B ▶ Now go to page 136. Look at the grammar chart and do the grammar exercise for 8.1.

C **PAIR WORK** Complete the sentences so that they are true for you. Then discuss your ideas with a partner. Do you like to do the same things?

1 When I'm on vacation, I love to … .
2 If the weather is nice on the weekend, I … .
3 When I travel long distances, I like to … .
4 I don't usually … when the weather is cold.

## 4 SPEAKING

A Imagine you're a host to some tourists. Think of places to take them in your town. You can go online for ideas. Where is the best place to take them …

- if they want to eat traditional food?
- if they want to see the sights?
- when it's cold or rainy?
- when it's very hot?
- if they're interested in funny or unusual sights?

B **GROUP WORK** Share your ideas with some of your classmates. Do you all agree?

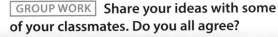

# TICKET TO RIDE

## 1 LANGUAGE IN CONTEXT

A  🔊 **2.11** **Journalist Rosalind Ash took a four-day bus trip from Brazil to Peru. Listen to her video. Which things from the list below does she talk about?**

**1** the food ☐       **2** reasons for taking the trip ☐       **3** other passengers ☐

🔊 **2.11 Audio script**

**DAY ONE**  I'm at Tietê bus station in São Paulo, in Brazil, to **catch the bus** for the long trip to Lima, Peru – *5,000* kilometers in *96* hours! It's going to be pretty amazing.

**DAY TWO**  We stopped for lunch at a roadside restaurant and **picked up more passengers**. I met Lucas, who's going to see his girlfriend. He'll **change buses** in Cáceres and go another 200 kilometers north. So many people, so many stories.

**DAY THREE**  It's 1:00 a.m., and we're high up in the mountains now. I think I'm the only person not asleep. Today I talked to a family with three young kids. They **take the bus** once a year to visit their grandparents. They bring a whole suitcase full of books and toys to keep the children happy. Smart parents!

**DAY FOUR**  Just 96 hours later, and we're in Lima! It's great to be here, and to **get off the bus**, but I feel a little sad that it's all over. It was a wonderful experience.

## 2 VOCABULARY: Using transportation

A  **Look at the words in bold in the video text above. Which picture, A, B, or C, do they describe? Write the words in the correct spaces. Can you find Rosalind? And Lucas? And the family she talks to?**

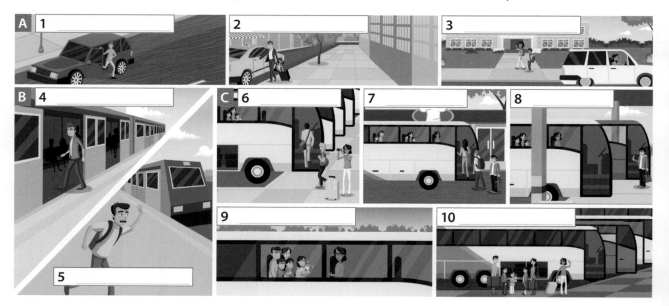

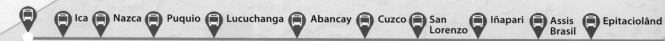

B   🔊 **2.12**   **Read the sentences and write the bold words in the other pictures on page 78. Listen and check your work.**

I **drop** the children **off** at school before I go to work.

When you **get into a taxi**, tell the driver where you want to go.

You can **get on the train** when the doors open.

If you **miss the train**, there's another one soon.

Check the traffic before you **get out of the car**.

C   ▶   **Now do the vocabulary exercises for 8.2 on page 148.**

D   **Would you like to take a four-day trip? Would you prefer to take a car, a bus, or a train? Where would you like to go? Why? You can go online for ideas.**

## 3   GRAMMAR: Giving reasons using *to* and *for*

A   (Circle) **the correct options to complete the rules. Use the sentences in the grammar box to help you. Underline the reasons in each sentence.**

To give reasons, you can use:

1   *to* + **verb** / **noun**      2   *for* + **verb** / **noun**

> **Giving reasons using *to* and *for***
>
> They take this trip once a year **to** visit their grandparents.
> They bring books and toys **to** keep the children happy.
> We stopped **for** lunch.

**✓ ACCURACY CHECK**

Don't use *for* before *to* + verb.

We went there ~~for~~ to pick up my sister! ✗
We went there to pick up my sister! ✓

B   ▶   **Now go to page 136. Look at the grammar chart and do the grammar exercise for 8.2.**

C   PAIR WORK   **Look at the questions. Write as many answers as you can using *to* + verb or *for* + noun. Check your accuracy. Tell another pair of students your answers.**

Why do you use public transportation? (*to go to school*, …)

Why do you go downtown? (*to go shopping*, …)

Why are you studying English? (*for my job*, …)

## 4   SPEAKING

A   **Describe a long trip you took some time in the past. Use the questions to help you prepare.**

- Where did you go?
- Why did you go there?
- How far was it?
- How long did it take?
- What form(s) of transportation did you take? Why?
- How did you feel when you arrived? Why?

B   PAIR WORK   **Work in pairs. Tell your partner about your journey. For ideas, watch Irene's video.**

I traveled from Bogotá to Caracas. I went to visit a friend and then we went to the coast together for a short vacation. I took the bus. It was a long bus ride!

**REAL STUDENT**

*Does Irene's trip sound fun to you?*

 Ji-Paraná    Vilhena    Pontes e Lacerda    Cáceres    Rondonópolis    Maracaí  

South Atlantic Ocean

São Paulo

# THAT'S A GREAT IDEA!

**LESSON OBJECTIVE**
- give advice and make suggestions

## 1 FUNCTIONAL LANGUAGE

A  🔊 **2.13** **Read and listen to two conversations. What do the tourists want to know?**

🔊 **2.13 Audio script**

**1**  **A** Hi. Tonight is our last night in your beautiful city. Any idea what we can do?

**B** Your last night? Well, **how about going** to the theater?

**A** We went to the theater last night.

**B** **Why don't you go** to the mall? There are some great cafés with live music.

**A** The mall! **That's a great idea.** How do we get there?

**B** It's not far – about ten blocks. I can take you there if you'd like.

**A** Thank you!

**2**  **A** Can you tell us how to get to the airport?

**B** What time is your flight?

**A** It's at 7:00 p.m. **Should** we **take** a taxi?

**B** **You could** use the hotel shuttle service. It leaves from here every 30 minutes.

**A** **That would be great**. How long does it take to get to the airport?

**B** It takes about 45 minutes. **You should take** the 3:00 p.m. shuttle to get there for 4:00 p.m.

**A** 3:00 p.m.? **Perfect**! We'll be here. Thanks!

B  **Complete the chart with expressions in bold from the conversations above.**

> **INSIDER** ENGLISH
>
> **Use *take* for time and for transportation.**
> *If you **take the bus**, it **takes 30 minutes**.*     *When you **take the subway**, it **takes 15**.*

| Giving advice and making suggestions | Responding to advice and suggestions |
|---|---|
| 1 _____ to (the theater)? | That's a great ⁶ _____ ! |
| 2 _____ to (the mall)? | That ⁷ _____ be great. |
| 3 _____ we take a taxi? | 3:00 p.m.? ⁸ _____ ! |
| 4 _____ use the hotel shuttle service. | |
| You ⁵ _____ take (the 3:00 p.m. shuttle). | |

C  PAIR WORK  **Practice the conversations in exercise 1A with your partner.**

## 2 REAL-WORLD STRATEGY

A  🔊 **2.14** **Listen to the hotel receptionist talk to another guest. What two things does she suggest? Which one does the hotel guest decide to do?**

### ECHO QUESTIONS

Use echo questions to ask someone to repeat specific information. In an echo question, you repeat the part of the sentence that you hear and then use a question word to ask for the information that you don't hear.

*The hotel shuttle to the airport leaves <u>every 30 minutes</u>.*

*Sorry, the hotel shuttle leaves **how often**?*

*There's a concert <u>in the park</u> tonight.*

*Wait, there's a concert **where**?*

B  🔊 **2.14** **Read the information about echo questions, above. Then look at the sentences from the conversation and complete the questions. Listen again and check.**

**A** How about going to the mall?

**B** Going ¹_____?

**A** You could go to the museum. It opens at 10:00, so you don't have long to wait.

**B** Wait, it opens ²_____?

C  ▶ | PAIR WORK | **Student A: Go to page 158. Student B: Go to page 160. Follow the instructions.**

## 3 PRONUNCIATION: Saying long and short vowel sounds

A  🔊 **2.15** **Listen. Which word sounds shorter? Which is the last sound in this word?**

**1** great            **2** grade

B  🔊 **2.16** **Listen and check (✓) the words that sound longer.**

**1** ☐ tried    ☐ flight          **3** ☐ art      ☐ award

**2** ☐ night    ☐ side           **4** ☐ need     ☐ meet

C  | PAIR WORK | **Practice the sentences with a partner.**

**1** I need to eat.

**2** Why don't we meet?

**3** We could meet in the street.

**4** How about meeting in the street for something to eat?

## 4 SPEAKING

A  **Imagine some tourists stop you on the street outside your home. They ask you for advice. Choose <u>one</u> of the situations below and think of two or three suggestions for the tourists.**

**1** They want to get to the main square downtown. They don't want to take a taxi.

**2** They need to go to the train station as quickly as possible.

**3** They're hungry and looking for a place to eat quickly and cheaply.

**4** They want to see the best parts, but they don't want to walk.

B  | PAIR WORK | **Student A: You are the tourist. Ask for help. Student B: Offer your advice. Student A: Respond to the suggestions. Then reverse the roles and use a different situation.**

**LESSON OBJECTIVE**
- write advice on living in another country

## 1 LISTENING

A **PAIR WORK** Imagine that a friend is leaving in six months to live in another country. What three pieces of advice can you give him/her? Discuss with your partner.

B 🔊 **2.17** **LISTEN FOR GIST** Listen to four people giving advice to people who are going to live in another country. Is their advice the same as yours?

C 🔊 **2.17** **LISTEN FOR DETAIL** Listen again. What advice does each caller give? Write 1, 2, 3, or 4.

1 Learn the language. ☐1☐
2 Get to know your way around with maps. ☐
3 Find a good place to live. ☐
4 Work with a conversation partner. ☐

5 Ask friends or family about local customs. ☐
6 Get to know people. ☐
7 Join clubs or groups that fit your interests. ☐

D **PAIR WORK** **THINK CRITICALLY** People don't always choose to move to another country. Think of reasons why people leave their home countries. What extra problems do they usually face?

## 2 PRONUNCIATION: Listening for intonation

A 🔊 **2.18** Listen. Focus on the rising intonation and falling intonation of the speaker's voice.

If you have any family friends or contacts in the country, ask them to help.

B 🔊 **2.19** Draw arrows to show the rising intonation ↗ and the falling intonation ↘. Listen and check.

1 When you join a language club, you can learn very quickly.

2 If you can, try and find a place before you go.

3 If you like hiking, join a hiking club.

C (Circle) the correct option to complete the sentence.

Speakers' voices often go up to show they're *finished / not finished*.

## 3 WRITING

A  Read the listeners' comments. What extra advice do they offer? Do you agree with the advice? Which do you think is the best advice?

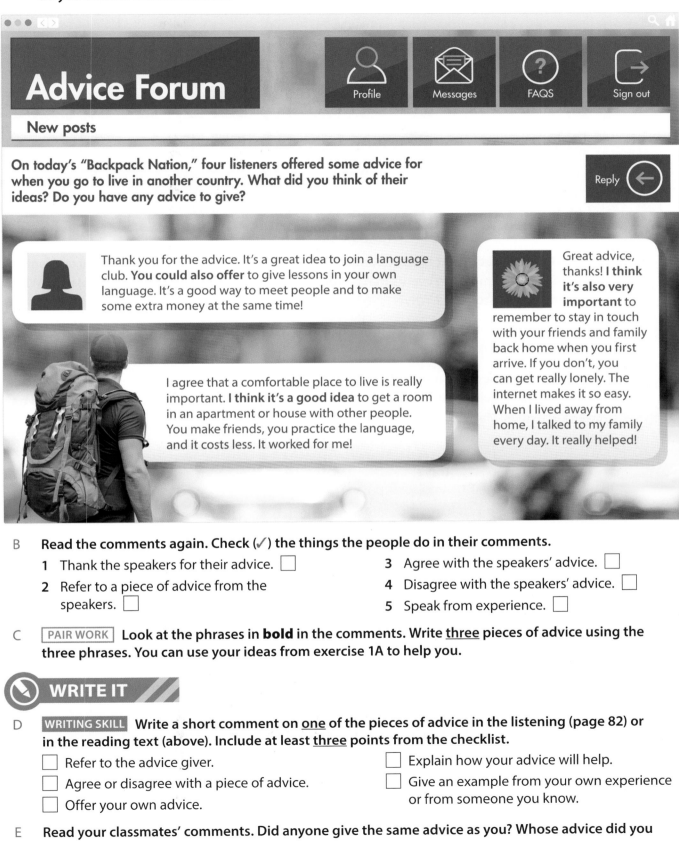

**Advice Forum**

Profile    Messages    FAQS    Sign out

**New posts**

On today's "Backpack Nation," four listeners offered some advice for when you go to live in another country. What did you think of their ideas? Do you have any advice to give?

Reply

Thank you for the advice. It's a great idea to join a language club. **You could also offer** to give lessons in your own language. It's a good way to meet people and to make some extra money at the same time!

Great advice, thanks! **I think it's also very important** to remember to stay in touch with your friends and family back home when you first arrive. If you don't, you can get really lonely. The internet makes it so easy. When I lived away from home, I talked to my family every day. It really helped!

I agree that a comfortable place to live is really important. **I think it's a good idea** to get a room in an apartment or house with other people. You make friends, you practice the language, and it costs less. It worked for me!

B  Read the comments again. Check (✓) the things the people do in their comments.

1  Thank the speakers for their advice. ☐
2  Refer to a piece of advice from the speakers. ☐
3  Agree with the speakers' advice. ☐
4  Disagree with the speakers' advice. ☐
5  Speak from experience. ☐

C  PAIR WORK  Look at the phrases in **bold** in the comments. Write <u>three</u> pieces of advice using the three phrases. You can use your ideas from exercise 1A to help you.

### WRITE IT

D  WRITING SKILL  Write a short comment on <u>one</u> of the pieces of advice in the listening (page 82) or in the reading text (above). Include at least <u>three</u> points from the checklist.

☐ Refer to the advice giver.
☐ Agree or disagree with a piece of advice.
☐ Offer your own advice.
☐ Explain how your advice will help.
☐ Give an example from your own experience or from someone you know.

E  Read your classmates' comments. Did anyone give the same advice as you? Whose advice did you like the most?

# TIME TO SPEAK
## Planning a trip

**A** **RESEARCH** Look at the pictures of popular tourist destinations. What types of places or events are they? Think of three more big events that people travel to. Why do people go to these places? Which place would you like to go to? Why?

**B** Choose a destination that you would all like to go to. Think of some different things to see. What activities would you like to do?

**C** **PREPARE** You are going on a trip for three days. Decide what you want to do on each day. Make sure you include activities for all the different tastes and interests of your group. Plan how you'll travel between activities. Make a table like the one below and take notes.

Destination: _____

|  | Travel | Activities | Things to see |
|---|---|---|---|
| Day 1 |  |  |  |
| Day 2 |  |  |  |
| Day 3 |  |  |  |

**D** **PRESENT** Tell the class about your plans. Listen to the other groups. Which vacations sound the most relaxing? The most active? The most fun? Which would you most like to go on? Why?

≫ *To check your progress, go to page 155.* ≫

# USEFUL PHRASES

**RESEARCH**
It looks like a …
What can we do there?

**PREPARE**
Let's go to …
What do you want to do there?
I suggest …
Why don't we eat/watch/play …

**PRESENT**
First, we …
After that … / Then … /
Next …
Finally …

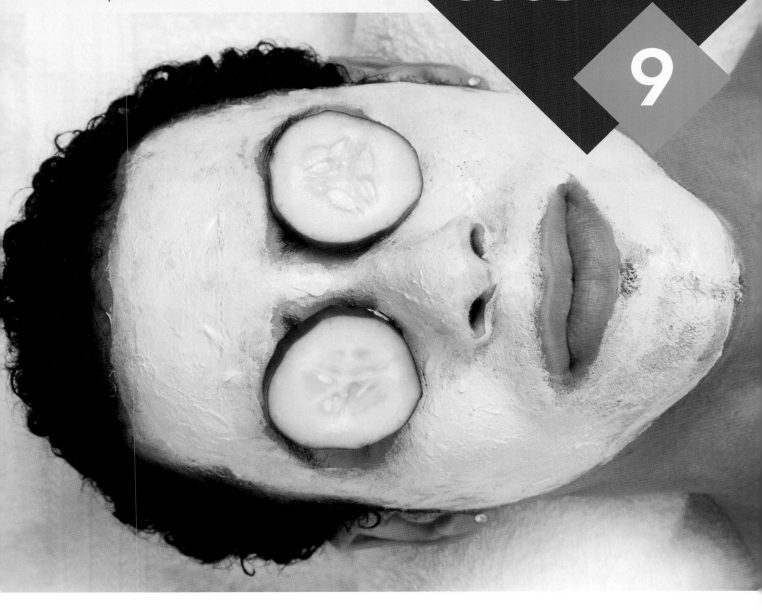

**UNIT OBJECTIVES**

- compare stores and what they sell
- talk about people in photos
- ask for and give opinions
- write a paragraph describing a photo
- create and present an ad

## START SPEAKING

A  **Look at the picture. What's he doing? Do you do this?**

B  **Think about yourself and your friends. Do you think a lot about the clothes you wear and how you look? How many times a day do you look at yourself (in mirrors, pictures, selfies, store windows, etc.)? For ideas, watch Alessandra's video.**

**REAL STUDENT**

*Are you the same as Alessandra?*

C  *A picture is worth a thousand words.* **What does this mean? Do you agree? Are pictures important to you? Why?**

# 9.1 WHAT TO WEAR AT WORK

## 1 VOCABULARY: Naming accessories

A 🔊 2.20 **PAIR WORK** **Listen and say the words. Which items do you have? Tell a partner.**

tie, belt, sunglasses, gloves, scarf, socks, sneakers, bracelets, earrings, necklace

B ▶ **Now do the vocabulary exercises for 9.1 on page 149.**

C **Put the accessories in order from head to feet. Do you and your partner agree on the order?**

## 2 LANGUAGE IN CONTEXT

A **Look at the pictures. What are they wearing? Now read an email from Mike to a friend. In the pictures, which one is Mike, and which one is his new coworker?**

Hi Angelica,

Well, here I am in Berlin! I still can't believe it – I had an interview one month ago, and I started work today!

So far, Europe's OK, very pretty. But the weather is worse than at home – colder, wetter, windier – horrible! 😖 For my first day on the job, I wore my winter suit with a blue **tie**.

I didn't know it, but the dress code at this company is a lot less formal than at my old company. **Sneakers** and T-shirts for almost everyone. A lot of the men wear **bracelets** and **earrings**! And everything is more modern than at my old office. The work is more or less the same, but the people are much warmer and friendlier than in my old office. Maybe it's the sneakers!

It's definitely a more interesting place to work, and the money is better, too.
I'm really lucky. But I'm going to need to buy some casual clothes!

Mike

**GLOSSARY**
**formal** (*adj*) traditional, serious
**casual** (*adj*) relaxed, not formal

B **Read the email again. Check (✓) the sentence(s) that are true. Correct the false ones.**

☐ 1 The new office is different from his old office.
☐ 2 The people in his new job aren't very friendly.
☐ 3 Some things in his new office aren't so good.
☐ 4 He prefers the weather in Berlin.

C **GROUP WORK** **What do business people usually wear to work where you live? Would you prefer to work in an office where appearance is important? Why? For ideas, watch Caio's video.**

REAL STUDENT
*Do you agree with Caio?*

## 3 GRAMMAR: Comparative adjectives

**A** **Answer the questions. Use the sentences in the grammar box to help you.**

1 Which word do you use after a comparative adjective to compare two or more things?
_____

2 What are the opposites of *more formal* and *less modern*?
_____  _____

3 What are the comparatives of *good* and *bad*?
_____  _____

> ### Comparative adjectives
>
> Everything is **more modern than** at my old office. The dress code is a lot **less formal**.
> The weather is **worse than** at home. The money is **better**.
> It's **colder, wetter, windier**.
>
> ! more => less = <

**B** ▶ **Now go to page 137. Look at the grammar chart and do the grammar exercise for 9.1.**

**C** **Put the adjectives in parentheses in the comparative form to make sentences that are true for you. Use *than* and *less* when necessary. Then check your accuracy.**

1 People usually look _____ in black clothes. (formal)

2 In winter, warm gloves are _____ a hat. (important)

3 A necklace is _____ a scarf. (expensive)

4 Colored sneakers are _____ white ones. (cool)

5 People look _____ when they wear ties. (serious)

✓ **ACCURACY** CHECK

Don't use *more* and *-er* together.
Your sunglasses are ~~more better~~ than mine. ✗
Your sunglasses are better than mine. ✓

**D** | PAIR WORK | **Do you agree with your partner's sentences in exercise 3C?**

> I think black is boring. I wear lots of different colors.

> Really? I think black is cool. It looks good on everyone!

## 4 SPEAKING

| GROUP WORK | **Think of two places in your town where you can buy clothes and fashion accessories. Go online for ideas if you want. Compare these places and the things they sell. Use the adjectives in the box or your own ideas.**

IND IT

| beautiful | cheap/expensive | fashionable | friendly | good/bad | interesting |

# 9.2 BABY PHOTOS

## 1 VOCABULARY: Describing appearance

A ◄ᴺ 2.21 **Listen and say the words.**

light hair | bald | dark, straight hair | curly gray hair
pierced ear | mustache | beard

B PAIR WORK **Imagine you're designing your own avatar. Use the features in exercise 1A. Describe your avatar to your partner. How is your avatar's appearance different from your real appearance?**

C ➤ **Now do the vocabulary exercises for 9.2 on page 149.**

D PAIR WORK **Think of a famous man and a famous woman. Describe them to your partner. Can they guess who you're describing? Now compare the two people (who has longer hair, darker hair, etc.).**

> She is a young woman with very long hair.

> Is her hair darker or lighter than the other person?

## 2 LANGUAGE IN CONTEXT

A PAIR WORK **Think about a picture of you as a child. Describe it to your partner.**

B ◄ᴺ 2.22 **Listen to the conversation between Pete, Pete's mom, and Pete's new girlfriend, Ava. Describe Pete's appearance as a baby and as a teenager. How does Pete feel about the photos now?**

### ◄ᴺ 2.22 Audio script

**Mom** Ava, would you like to see some pictures of Pete when he was younger?

**Pete** Mom, please …

**Mom** Look. This one is when Pete was two. Isn't he the cutest little baby with his **dark**, **straight hair** and funny smile?

**Ava** Yes!

**Mom** This is the funniest one. He was 15, and he had a little **mustache**. He couldn't grow a real **beard**, of course. He was the youngest boy in the class, but you wanted to look older. He was the most sensitive child.

**Pete** Mom, why do you always want to show people the worst pictures of me?

**Mom** Now, where is my favorite one, you know, from when you were 12 months old? You in the bath. It's here somewhere …

**Pete** No, not that one, Mom. Please …

**Mom** Here it is! It's the best one of all!

**Pete** Oh, no.

88

## 3 GRAMMAR: Superlative adjectives

A  (Circle) the correct options to complete the rules. Use the sentences in the grammar box to help you.

1  Superlative adjectives usually begin with *a / the*.

2  Superlatives compare **two things / three or more things**.

3  Short superlatives end with *-er / -est*. Longer superlatives begin with *the most / more*.

4  The superlative of *good* is **the best / the worst**. The superlative of *bad* is **the best / the worst**.

---

**Superlative adjectives**

Isn't he **the cutest** little baby?

He was **the most sensitive** child.

Why do you always want to show people **the worst** pictures of me?

This is **the best** one of all.

---

B  ▶ Now go to page 137. Look at the grammar chart and do the grammar exercise for 9.2.

C  | PAIR WORK |  **Put the adjectives in parentheses in the superlative form. Then answer the questions and give some details about each person. Tell your partner.**

Which of your friends or family members has …

1  the _____ eyes? (beautiful)

2  the _____ beard? (big)

3  the _____ makeup? (cool)

4  the _____ hair? (curly)

5  the _____ hair? (dark)

6  the _____ smile? (friendly)

7  the _____ clothes? (good)

8  the _____ jewelry? (interesting)

> My cousin Ramon has the best clothes. He always wears sunglasses and cool shoes.

## 4 SPEAKING

IND IT

| PAIR WORK |  **Find three pictures of the same person (you or another person) on your phone. Show the pictures to your partner and give an opinion about each one using superlatives. Does your partner agree?**

> Here are three pictures of me. I think this is the best one. I like it because I have a happy smile and my hair looks good. It's a picture of me on vacation at the beach last year. That was the most fantastic vacation of my life. What do you think? Is this the best of the pictures?

# WHAT DO YOU THINK OF THIS?

## 1 FUNCTIONAL LANGUAGE

A 🔊 **2.23** **Read and listen to the conversations. What are the people making decisions about?**

**INSIDER ENGLISH**

Use *go with* to say that two things match.
*Does this belt **go with** these pants?*

🔊 **2.23 Audio script**

**1** A **What do you think of** this scarf, Sam?

B **It looks nice**, Fiona! Really nice.

A **Don't you think it's** kind of bright?

B It's a little bright, **I guess**, but not too much. And it goes with your dress.

A **How do you feel about** this white one?

B **I prefer** the other one.

A This one?

B Yes. **It's perfect**! And it's cheaper, too.

**2** A I'm thinking of using this picture for my blog. **Do you like it**?

B **I'm not sure**. You don't seem very happy.

A I'm smiling in the photo! How about this one?

B **That one is** better, but **isn't it** a little formal?

A Really? Can you look and choose the best one?

B Sure.

B **Complete the chart with expressions in bold from the conversations above.**

| Asking for an opinion | Giving a positive opinion | Giving a negative or neutral opinion |
|---|---|---|
| What do you ¹_____ this? | It ⁴_____ nice. | Don't you ⁸_____ it's (kind of bright)? |
| How do you feel ²_____? | I ⁵_____ the other one. | I ⁹_____. |
| Do you ³_____ it? | It's ⁶_____! | I'm not ¹⁰_____. |
| | ⁷_____ is better. | ¹¹_____ it (a little formal)? |

C **PAIR WORK** **Practice the conversations in exercise 1A with a partner.**

## 2 REAL-WORLD STRATEGY

A  🔊 **2.24** **Listen to another conversation between Sam and Fiona. What item is Fiona trying to choose?**

B  🔊 **2.24** **Complete Fiona's opinion of Sam's suggestion below. Listen again and check. Is her opinion positive?**

**Sam**    How do you feel about these?        **Fiona**    They're OK, _____ .

> **I GUESS**
>
> Use *I guess* when you're not certain about something or if you don't have a strong opinion.
> *Don't you think these shoes go perfectly with this dress?*
> *I guess, but I like your brown sandals with it, too.*

C  🔊 **2.25**  **PAIR WORK**  **Read the information about *I guess* in the box above. Then write it in the correct places in the conversations below. Listen and check. Then practice the sentences with a partner.**

1  A  I think these earrings are great _____ .
   B  They're OK, _____ I guess _____ .

2  A  This belt is OK, _____ . But it's nothing special.
   B  _____ I think it's perfect.

3  A  You look really serious in that picture _____ . I prefer this one.
   B  Yeah, _____ it's better than the other one.

## 3 PRONUNCIATION: Saying /ɜ/ vowel sound

A  🔊 **2.26** **Listen. Underline the parts of the words with the /ɜ/ vowel sound.**

1  pref<u>er</u>       2  shirt       3  perfect

B  **PAIR WORK**  **Say one of the words in each group. Your partner listens and circle the word you say. Then switch roles.**

1  **a**  bird  **b**  bed        2  **a**  turn  **b**  ten        3  **a**  heard  **b**  head

C  🔊 **2.27** **Underline the words with the /ɜ/ sound. Listen and check, and practice the conversation with a partner.**

A  What do you think of this red shirt?        B  Turn around … Hmm, I'm not sure.
A  How do you feel about this green shirt?        B  I prefer the first shirt.

## 4 SPEAKING

**GROUP WORK**  **Look at the pictures and discuss your opinions. Use the functional language to help you.**

> What do you think of that shirt?

> I think it's awful! I prefer the one on the right. How do you feel about that one?

> It's kind of fun, I guess.

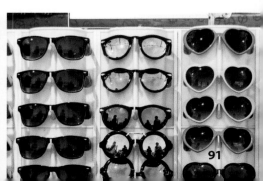

# IMAGE IS EVERYTHING

## 1 READING

A **THINK BEFORE YOU READ** Look at the pictures from different car ads. What do the pictures say about the cars? Which images do you like the most?

B **READ FOR MAIN IDEAS** Look at the different types of people and match them to the pictures in exercise 1A. Then read the article and match the people to the paragraphs.

a The happy family     c The cool city person

b The driver of the future     d The freedom lover

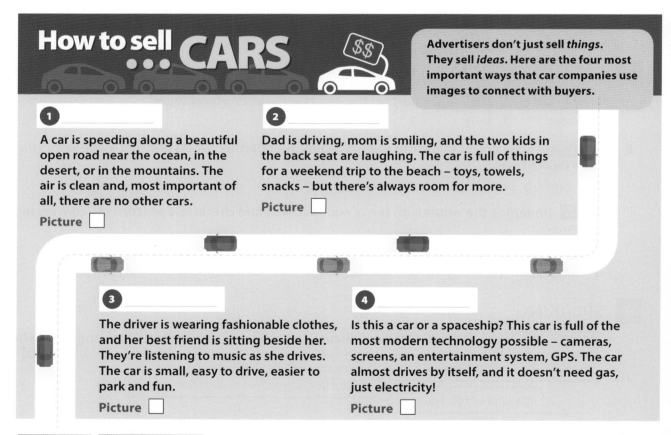

## How to sell ... CARS $$

Advertisers don't just sell *things*. They sell *ideas*. Here are the four most important ways that car companies use images to connect with buyers.

**1** _____

A car is speeding along a beautiful open road near the ocean, in the desert, or in the mountains. The air is clean and, most important of all, there are no other cars.

Picture ☐

**2** _____

Dad is driving, mom is smiling, and the two kids in the back seat are laughing. The car is full of things for a weekend trip to the beach – toys, towels, snacks – but there's always room for more.

Picture ☐

**3** _____

The driver is wearing fashionable clothes, and her best friend is sitting beside her. They're listening to music as she drives. The car is small, easy to drive, easier to park and fun.

Picture ☐

**4** _____

Is this a car or a spaceship? This car is full of the most modern technology possible – cameras, screens, an entertainment system, GPS. The car almost drives by itself, and it doesn't need gas, just electricity!

Picture ☐

C **PAIR WORK** **THINK CRITICALLY** Discuss the ways that the car ads in the article are different from reality. Look at the ideas in the box and add two more.

*Some families are not happy on long car trips.*
*It's often difficult to find any parking space, big or small.*

## 2 WRITING

A Read the information about a contest. Then read the email below. Which kind of customer is this image for? Do you like this person's idea? Why or why not?

**ADVERTISING CONTEST!**

We are looking for the perfect image for an ad for our new car, and we need YOUR help!

**What image do you suggest?**

Email your best idea to best_car_ad@carwars.com.

Describe your idea in 50–80 words. Your image can be a photo or a drawing. The winner gets a free CAR!

● ● ● ‹ ›                                                                    Reply   Forward

The car is in a street where people live. It's a small car, perfect for the city. Someone is cleaning the car. He or she is very proud of it. The idea is that the car is very important to the person because it's very practical, but it also looks good.

B Read another submission to the contest. Divide the text into four sentences with correct punctuation. Check your work by looking at exercise 2A. What kind of customer are these images for?

my image is of a beach on a warm summer day the car is parked and the driver is getting beach things out of the back the driver's door is open and her dog is already running to the beach this image gives the idea of being young and full of energy

C WRITING SKILLS Look at these other submissions. The sentences are too long, and the writers did not use any periods. Change the texts into two or three sentences. Don't forget the capital letters.

1 the most important thing in my image is the famous football player next to the car he is standing with a football in one hand and the key to the car in the other

2 my image shows an open door of the car you can see the inside of the car it looks very modern and nice

D Prepare your ideas for the contest. Describe your image. Use these phrases to help you.

*My image shows …*                          *The car is driving on a …*

*The most important thing in my image is …*  *There are no other cars in the image …*

E GROUP WORK Share your submission and image with the rest of the class. Which images and ideas do you like most?

# TIME TO SPEAK
## Sell it!

**A**   **RESEARCH**   Look at the pictures. What do you see? What do you think they are selling?

**B**   **DISCUSS**   Here are some of the most popular people and things in advertisements. Why do you think they are popular? Use the phrases at the bottom of the page to help you.

- animals
- babies and children
- perfect families
- friends having fun
- beautiful people
- funny or romantic stories

**C**   **DECIDE**   Look at the list of products and agree on the two most interesting ones.

| | | |
|---|---|---|
| an airline | candy | jeans |
| perfume | a smartphone | soda |

**D**   **PREPARE**   Choose one of your products and make an ad for it. The ad can be print (magazine, poster) or a video (for TV or online). Think about these questions as you plan it.

- Who is the ad for? (parents, teenagers, etc.)
- Who is in the ad? What are they wearing?
- Where is the ad? (in the mountains, in a house, etc.)
- What happens in the ad?
- What do the people say?
- What kind of music is in the ad?
- Are there words in the ad? What do they say?

**E**   **PRESENT**   Present your ad to the class. When all the presentations are finished, have an awards ceremony. Vote on the best ads in these categories:

- the funniest ad
- the most interesting ad
- the most creative ad
- the best ad

>> *To check your progress, go to page 155.* >>

---

# USEFUL PHRASES

 **DISCUSS**
In my opinion … / I'd say that …
I love ads with … because …
I think those ads are funny/cute/annoying/stupid.

 **DECIDE**
Let's do/choose/think about …
I think we should …

 **PRESENT**
Our ad starts with …
People are going to remember our ad because …

# REVIEW 3 (UNITS 7–9)

## 1 VOCABULARY

A **Complete the chart with words from the box.**

| burger | bus station | gloves | onion | roasted | scarf | spicy | suitcase |

| cereal | bitter | airplane | belt |
|---|---|---|---|
| chicken | boiled | backpack | bracelet |
| jam | delicious | check-in | earrings |
| lettuce | grilled | guidebook | necklace |
| strawberry | sour | map | tie |
| 1 _____ | 3 _____ | 5 _____ | 7 _____ |
| 2 _____ | 4 _____ | 6 _____ | 8 _____ |

B **Write a category for each group of words above. Then add at least two more words or phrases to each group.**

## 2 GRAMMAR

A **Complete the conversation.**

**A** Excuse me, can you help me? I can't find my little sister, Nell. I went to the café ¹*for / to* a burger and ²*a / some* fries for us. Nell wanted ³*for / to* stay outside. She always waits for me ⁴*where / when* I go somewhere. Normally, she doesn't mind ⁵*be / being* alone for a ⁶*some / few* minutes. But now I can't find her.

**B** It's all right. I'll help you. Describe her to me.

**A** Well, she's ten years old. She has dark hair – it's longer ⁷*for / than* mine, and it's ⁸*curlier / curliest*. She's wearing jeans and a pink T-shirt. It's ⁹*more / the most* colorful T-shirt you can imagine! Oh, and she doesn't speak ¹⁰*some / any* English.

**B** Don't worry. A lot ¹¹*the / of* children get lost, and we always find them. The ¹²*better / best* thing to do is wait here. I'm going to contact the security officers, OK?

B  PAIR WORK  **Practice reading the conversation with a partner. Change the details and make a new conversation.**

## 3 SPEAKING

A  PAIR WORK  **Think of a special place that you enjoy going to -- a park, a shopping mall, an amusement park, etc. Work with a partner and discuss the questions. Make notes on your partner's answers.**

■ Why do you enjoy going there? What do you like to do there?

■ Can you think of three different reasons that people go to this place?

■ When you go to this place, what are the first things you do?

■ Is it very close to your home? What is the easiest way to get there?

■ Is it better to go on the weekend or during the week? Why? What is the best time of day to go?

> I like to go to a little park near the river. It's a good place for…

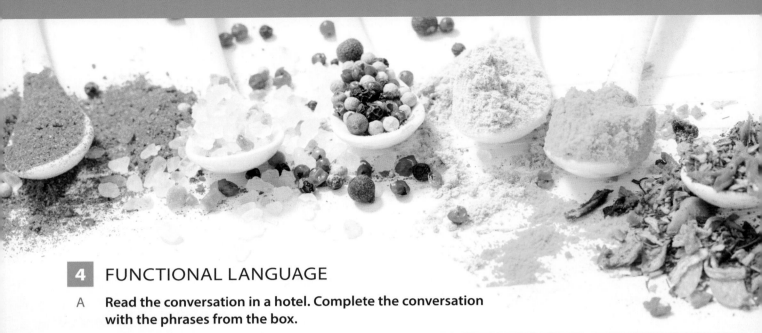

## 4 FUNCTIONAL LANGUAGE

A  **Read the conversation in a hotel. Complete the conversation with the phrases from the box.**

| could you recommend | how about | how was it | I'd like | if you want, you can |
|---|---|---|---|---|
| I guess | we prefer | what do you think | what kind of | you could |

**A** Excuse me, ¹_____ a place for dinner?

**B** Sure. ²_____ food do you like?

**A** It doesn't matter to my husband, but I think ³_____ something Italian.

**B** Well, ⁴_____ try the pizzeria across the street, or ⁵_____ eat at the hotel restaurant. We have pasta dishes.

**A** ⁶_____ of the pizzeria? Is it good?

**B** It's okay, ⁷_____, but I think the hotel restaurant is better.

**A** ⁸_____ somewhere different. We ate here yesterday.

**B** Well, there's Bella Napoli, that new Italian place near the park. I went there last week. ⁹_____ that?

**A** ¹⁰_____ ?

**B** It was really nice.

B  PAIR WORK  **Practice reading the conversation in pairs. Then change the details to make a new conversation.**

## 5 SPEAKING

A  PAIR WORK  **Choose one of the situations. Act it out in pairs.**

1  You are preparing a dish that you really like. Tell your friend about the dish. Then ask for an opinion and advice. Your friend suggests ways of improving it.

   **A** Here, taste this. What do you think?

   **B** Mm, delicious! And very spicy.

2  You brought your friend to your family's celebration. All your favorite foods are there. Tell your friend about the foods and say which are the best, and why. Answer your friend's questions, too.

   **A** My grandmother makes the most delicious desserts.

   **B** I love sweet things! What's in this one? …

B  **Change roles and repeat the role play.**

**UNIT OBJECTIVES**
- talk about how to avoid danger at work
- make predictions about your future
- describe a medical problem and ask for help
- write an email to your future self
- plan a reality TV show

# RISKY BUSINESS

# 10

## START SPEAKING

A   What can you see in the picture? Would you like to do this? Why or why not?

B   Which of these dangerous or scary things do you enjoy? Think of three more things.

| | | |
|---|---|---|
| amusement parks | dark places | extreme sports |
| fast cars | horror movies | |

C   What things are you afraid of? For ideas, watch Celeste's video.

**REAL STUDENT**

*Are you afraid of the same things as Celeste?*

# 10.1 DANGER ON THE JOB

**LESSON OBJECTIVE**
- talk about how to avoid danger at work

## 1 VOCABULARY: Describing jobs

A 🔊 **2.28** **PAIR WORK** Listen and repeat the jobs. Which ones are the most dangerous?

| | | | | |
|---|---|---|---|---|
| accountant | architect | call center worker | dentist | engineer |
| IT specialist | lawyer | mechanic | nurse | paramedic |
| photographer | physical therapist | police officer | project manager | receptionist |

B 🔊 **2.29** Which jobs from the list in exercise 1A are in the pictures? Label them. Then listen and check.

C ▶ Now do the vocabulary exercises for 10.1 on page 150.

## 2 LANGUAGE IN CONTEXT

A Look at the title of the article. Which jobs in exercise 1A is it talking about? Read and check your answers.

B **GROUP WORK** Think of (a) a person you know who has one of the jobs in exercise 1A and (b) a person who has a dangerous job. Is it the same person? Do they like their job(s)? Why or why not?

---

**GLOSSARY**
**microbe** (*n*) a tiny life form, including bacteria, viruses, and fungi.
**square inch** (*n*) a unit of measurement. 1 in² = 6.5 cm².

● ● ● ‹ › ›

# DANGER AT WORK!

I'm an office worker. I spend my working life at my computer. It's not physically difficult, but it's not without danger. Dr. Charles Gerba, a germ expert from the University of Arizona, says there are millions of invisible enemies all around us ...

**A** Viruses love offices. Air-conditioning systems recycle air and the germs in it. When one person in the office has a cold, their germs are on 40–60% of their coworkers in just four hours. The virus can stay in the office for three days!

**B** Some keyboards are dirtier than toilet seats – fact! Dr. Gerba did a study of more than 100 offices (law offices, call centers, accountant services, etc.) and found keyboards with 3,295 microbes per square inch. For toilet seats, that number is usually about 49 microbes!

Why? Food falls into your keyboard and produces bacteria. Dr. Gerba calls the keyboard a "bacteria cafeteria." Next lunchtime, ask yourself: "Do I really have to eat at my desk?"

## 3   GRAMMAR: *have to*

A   (Circle) the options to complete the sentences. Use the sentences in the grammar box to help you. Match each point to a paragraph in the article on page 98.

1   It **is / isn't** necessary to clean your keyboard. ___

2   It **is / isn't** necessary to stay home when you have a cold. ___

> **have to**
>
> a   You **have to** clean your keyboard.
>
> b   You **don't have to** stay home when you have a cold, but it's better if you do.

B   ▶   **Now go to page 138. Look at the grammar chart and do the grammar exercise for 10.1.**

C   Complete the questions with the correct form of *have to*. Then check your accuracy. Ask your partner the questions and take notes. Then tell a new partner about your first partner's answers.

1   you / work / long hours? How many hours / you / work?

*Do you have to work long hours? How many hours do you have to work?*

2   What time / you / start / work?

3   you / wear / special clothes? Why?

4   What kind of dangers / you / face / in your work?

5   you / get / any special training? What kind?

> ✓ **ACCURACY** CHECK
>
> The negative form is *don't / doesn't have to*.
> Use *do / does* in short answers.
>
> I don't have to go to school today.
> Really? I ~~have~~. ✗
> I don't have to go to school today.
> Really? I do. ✓

## 4   SPEAKING

GROUP WORK   **Think of a dangerous job that was <u>not</u> in this lesson. What dangers do people with this job have? What can they do to make their job safer? You can use your phone to find pictures and information.**

ND IT

> *Zookeepers have to work with dangerous animals. They have to clean up after the animals. To be safer, they have to put the animals in another place when they clean.*

# DON'T WORRY, DAD

**LESSON OBJECTIVE**
- make predictions about your future

## 1 VOCABULARY: Describing health problems

A 🔊 **2.30** **Listen and say the phrases. Find the problems in the pictures, circle them, and draw a line to the correct phrase.**

break your leg / twist your ankle

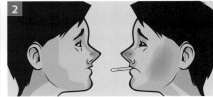
catch a cold / the flu

cut your finger / yourself shaving

have a headache / toothache / stomachache

have a fever / sore throat

hurt your back / bang your head

B **PAIR WORK** **Put the health problems in exercise 1A into two groups: INJURY (something that happens because of an accident) and ILLNESS (a way to be sick).**

C ▶ **Now do the vocabulary exercises for 10.2 on page 150.**

## 2 LANGUAGE IN CONTEXT

A 🔊 **2.31** **Amelia's father is worried about her. Listen and say why.**

**🔊 2.31 Audio script**

| | |
|---|---|
| **Father** | Are you ready, Amelia? Do you have everything? Will you be OK? |
| **Amelia** | Dad, I'm going to work, not the moon. I'll be fine. |
| **Father** | But it's your first day in a new job. Do you have your headache pills? You might have a headache later. Or hurt your back. I mean, all day in front of a computer. |
| **Amelia** | I won't need anything, Dad. |
| **Father** | How do you know? A new job, new people, new everything. It's a stressful situation. You might need something for that. |
| **Amelia** | It's a new experience, that's all. |
| **Father** | Will they give you anything to eat? You'll have a stomachache if you don't eat. And you'll probably be tired later in the day. Here's an energy drink. |
| **Amelia** | Thanks, Dad. |
| **Father** | Be careful! |
| **Amelia** | Love you, Dad! |

B 🔊 **2.31** **Listen again and read. Which health problems from exercise 1A does Amelia's father worry about?**

C  PAIR WORK  **Think of someone (a friend or a member of your family) who worries a lot. Give examples of things they say.**

## 3  GRAMMAR: Making predictions

A  **Complete the rules. Use the sentences in the grammar box to help you.**

1  We use *will* / _____ to make predictions about the future.

2  When we are not sure, we use _____ or _____ .

| Making predictions | |
|---|---|
| **Will** you be OK? | You **might** have a headache later. |
| I**'ll** be fine. | You **may** need something for that. |
| I **won't** need anything. | |

B  ▶ **Now go to page 138. Look at the grammar chart and do the grammar exercise for 10.2.**

C  PAIR WORK  **Read the situations and make <u>three</u> predictions for each one using the words in the box.**

| may | maybe | might | possibly | probably | will/'ll | won't |
|---|---|---|---|---|---|---|

1  It's Silvia's first day in her new job in a call center. She has a headache, and feels stressed.

_____

2  Benny has a stomachache and a fever. He has an important job interview later in the day.

_____

3  Vera is running to work because she's late. It's very cold and there's snow on the ground.

_____

## 4  SPEAKING

A  **You're going to ask a partner to make predictions about his/her future. Prepare your questions.
Use the topics in the box or your own ideas.**

| family life | health | home | studies | work |
|---|---|---|---|---|

Five years from now, do you think you'll live in a house or an apartment?

When will you retire from work?

B  PAIR WORK  **Ask your questions from exercise 4A. Listen to your partner's answers. Say something positive about your partner's predictions. For ideas, watch Caio's video.**

**REAL STUDENT**

*Which predictions are more positive: Caio's or your partner's?*

I think I'll live in an apartment. I won't have enough money to buy a house.

Well, maybe your apartment will be big and really nice.

## 10.3 WHAT'S THE MATTER?

### 1  FUNCTIONAL LANGUAGE

A  🔊 **2.32**  **Read and listen to the conversations. What does the person need in each conversation?**

🔊 **2.32 Audio script**

**1**  **A**  **What's wrong?**

**B**  I really don't feel well, Anna. It feels like my throat is blocked.

**A**  **What's the matter?** Are you allergic to something?

**B**  No. It's my asthma. I can't breathe. **My chest hurts**.

**A**  **What do you want me to do?**

**B**  I need my inhaler. **Can you** get it for me?

**A**  Where is it?

**B**  It's on my desk.

**A**  Yes, sure. I'll be right back.

**2**  **A**  Good morning, ma'am. **How can I help** you?

**B**  **I need** something for my head.

**A**  **Where exactly does it hurt**?

**B**  **It hurts here** at the front. It's like something is squeezing my head. And **I have a pain** behind my eyes, too.

**A**  **What happened**? Did you bang your head or have an accident?

**B**  No, nothing like that. It's just a headache, but the pain is killing me.

**A**  OK. I can give you some tablets. Take two of these every four hours.

**INSIDER** ENGLISH

*The pain is killing me = It hurts a lot.*

B  **Complete the chart with expressions in bold from the conversations above.**

| Offering help | Asking for information about the problem | Asking someone for help |
|---|---|---|
| ¹ _____ I help you? | What's ³ _____ ? | ⁷ _____ get it for me? |
| ² _____ want me to do? | What's the ⁴ _____ ? | ⁸ _____ something (for my head). |
|  | Where exactly ⁵ _____ |  |
|  | _____ ? |  |
|  | What ⁶ _____ ? |  |

| Describing symptoms |
|---|
| My (chest) ⁹ _____ .   It ¹⁰ _____ here.   I have a ¹¹ _____ behind my eyes. |

C  **PAIR WORK**  **Practice the conversations in exercise 1A with your partner.**

## 2 REAL-WORLD STRATEGY

A 🔊 **2.33** Listen to another conversation in a drugstore. What is the customer's problem? Why does he have this problem?

B 🔊 **2.33** Read the information about how to describe pain, below. Listen to the conversation again and check (✓) the expression the customer uses to describe his pain. Write the complete phrase the customer uses.

> ### IT'S LIKE / IT FEELS LIKE
> When we're not sure about a medical problem or don't know the name of it, we can say *it is like* or *it feels like* something else.
>
> ☐ It's like _____
> ☐ It feels _____

C **Rearrange the words to make sentences.**
1 a / in / It's / knife / like / my stomach _____
2 a / bright / eyes / in / It's / light / like / my _____
3 broken / feels / It / like / it's _____
4 feels / hit / It / like / me / someone _____

## 3 PRONUNCIATION: Saying final consonant sounds

A 🔊 **2.34** Say these sounds together. Then listen and say the words.
1 /s/ and /t/ = /st/      3 /n/ and /d/ = /nd/      5 /k/ and /t/ = /kt/
2 /s/ and /k/ = /sk/      4 /n/ and /s/ = /ns/      6 /t/ and /s/ = /ts/

B 🔊 **2.35** Listen. Focus on the ends of the words. Which word has the same final consonant sound as the example word? (Circle) it.
1 *chest*:   (stressed)   exercised       4 *ambulance*:   experience   accident
2 *desk*:    twist        risk            5 *blocked*:     architect    dentist
3 *happened*: accountant  weekend         6 *hurts*:       sports       cleaned

C **PAIR WORK** Work with a partner. Practice the conversations. Focus on the final consonant sounds.
1 **A** What happe**ned**? Did you have an accide**nt**?       2 **A** It feels like my throat is blo**cked**.
  **B** No, nothing like that. My che**st** hur**ts**.              **B** Should I call an ambula**nce**?

## 4 SPEAKING

**PAIR WORK** Choose a medical problem from this unit. Then follow the instructions below.

**Student A:** You have a medical problem. Ask for help and explain what is wrong with you and what happened.

**Student B:** You see someone who is not well. Ask them about their problem, what happened, and how you can help.

Begin your role plays like this:

**A** *Are you OK? What's the matter?*          **B** *I'm not sure, I think ....*

# FACE YOUR FEARS

## 1 READING

A **PAIR WORK** Decibels (dB) tell us if a sound is loud or quiet. Look at the decibel scale and the list of sounds. Where does each sound go on the scale? Why is *85 dB* red?

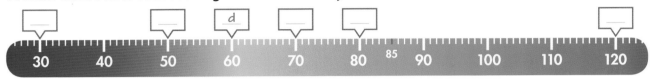

30    40    50    60    70    80    85    90    100    110    120

a breathing
b city traffic

c normal conversation
d office noise

e restaurant noise
f rock concert

B **PREDICT** Look at the title of the article. Why do you think Janet Horvath is afraid of sound?

C **READ FOR MAIN IDEAS** Read the article and check your answer. How does Janet face her fears?

# A Musician Afraid of Sound

It's 2011 and my husband can't kiss me. The smallest touch hurts me. Everyday noises – a baby crying, the sound of an ATM – are very painful. I'm a professional musician, but I can't stand sound.

It was August 2006. I was a cellist for the Minnesota Orchestra. There were eight speakers on stage. Two of them were too close to my left ear. When I left the stage, I felt a pain in my ears. It went down my neck and into my face. It was terrible. Later, my doctor told me I had a permanent injury from being so close to loud speakers, and my brain was now extremely sensitive to all sound. That meant no TV, no radio, no phone. And, worst of all, no music. It was the worst thing in the world that the thing I loved so much – music – now gave me so much pain.

But I didn't want to give up my career. I loved the cello – it was my life. I had to try to play the cello again.

I had to face my fears. I got a hearing device, and I slowly taught my brain to receive sound again. I can now play with three or four other musicians in a room. I won't be in an orchestra again, but I'll never be without music.

*Adapted from an article by musician Janet Horvath in* The Atlantic *magazine*

**GLOSSARY**
**sensitive** (*adj*) easily affected or damaged by physical activity or effect.
**device** (*n*) a small machine

D **READ FOR DETAILS** Read the article again and find …
1 Two examples of everyday noises that hurt Janet.
2 Four things she thought she had to live without.
3 One thing (of the four in number 2) that she didn't want to live without.
4 Two things Janet did to play the cello again.

E **PAIR WORK** **THINK CRITICALLY** How many decibels do you think the music from the speakers was? What noisy situations do you experience every day? How many are dangerously high? What can you do to protect your ears from high-decibel sounds?

## 2 WRITING

A   **Adam is writing an email to himself on a website that will deliver his email to him five years in the future. What is Adam afraid of? What's his advice to himself?**

---

Reply   Forward

**To:**
**From:**
**Subject:** Hello from the past

---

Hello you! Or really, hello ME, but five years in the future.

It's July 20 and it's 2:03 p.m. I'm 25 years old. When I read this email again, I'll be 30.

I'm writing this email because I want to read about what I was afraid of when I wrote it. And I hope that when I read it in five years, I'll see that everything is OK, that I'm OK.

So, what am I afraid of? I'm afraid of starting a new life in the city. I'm afraid because I don't know anyone, and I'm worried that I won't make any friends, and that I won't be successful in my new career.

I'm leaving a pretty good life. I live with my family in a great apartment. It's home. When I move to the city this fall, where will I live? Who will my friends be? Will I have any friends? Does it all work out well for me? Also, is my hair long, like I want it to be?

**Anyway**, I really just want to say that I trust you, … me, … us. It's a scary step to take, but it's for the best. You're smart and friendly, you're good at making the best of every situation. Don't be afraid that you made the wrong choice. You have to live your life and take chances! No matter what, it was a good choice.

**By the way**, you're still looking good. For 30.

Good luck with everything!

Adam (25 years old)

---

B   **WRITING SKILLS** **Look at the phrases in bold in the email. When do you use them? Complete the sentences.**

1   To return to the main idea of what you're saying, use _____ .

2   To say something new but connected to the main idea, use _____ .

C   **PAIR WORK** **What things are you afraid of? Choose from the word cloud. Compare with a partner. Do you have the same fears?**

## WRITE IT

D   **Think about your answers from exercise 2C and write an email to your future self.**

E   **GROUP WORK** **Share your emails. Do people have similar fears?**

# 10.5

## TIME TO SPEAK
### Reality TV

**A** What is reality TV? What reality TV shows are most popular at the moment? Do you watch them? Do you like them? Why or why not?

FIND IT

**B** **RESEARCH** Look at the different kinds of reality TV programs. Think of an example of each. What other types of reality shows do you know? Do you think any of these shows are dangerous? Why or why not? You can use your phone to help you.

**C** **DISCUSS** Work in small groups. Read the announcement. Brainstorm ideas for a new reality show. Use the questions and the useful phrases below to help you.

- Where will your show be?
- How many people will be on the show? Who will the people be?
- What do the people have to do?
- What "element of danger" will your show have?
- What will make your show exciting to watch?

## NEW REALITY SHOW
### *your ideas wanted!*

**BIG DEAL PRODUCTIONS**, a local TV production company, is accepting ideas for the next big reality show. The show has to have an element of danger, lots of people, and fun situations. Here is your chance to get creative and get on TV!!

**D** **PREPARE** Prepare a short presentation to the television company producers. Divide your presentation into sections that address the questions in exercise C.

**E** **PRESENT** Present your show to the producers (the class). Each person in the group should present a part. Then vote on which show is the best in general. Which is the most exciting? Which show is the most dangerous?

To check your progress, go to page 156.

# USEFUL PHRASES

**DISCUSS**
What do you think of … ?
I prefer …
I think we should …

**PREPARE**
Let's do/choose/think about …
We can talk about …

**PRESENT**
Our show will be in …
The contestants will have to …
It will be exciting to watch because …

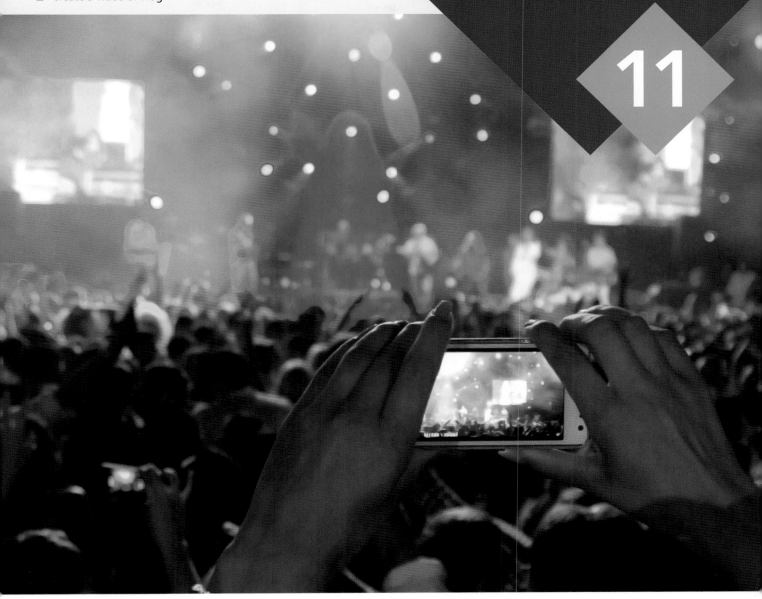

## UNIT OBJECTIVES

- talk about what you've done and what you've never done
- talk about what you've done, and when
- make and respond to requests
- write comments about an infographic
- create a video or vlog

# ME, ONLINE

# 11

## START SPEAKING

A   **What can you see in the picture? What are the people doing? Do you do this? Do you like it when other people do this?**

B   **What other types of screens can you add to the list below? How do you use these screens in your life?**

> ATM    computer    GPS    smartphone    tablet    TV

C   **Do you like sharing your photos and videos online? Why or why not? For ideas, watch Irene's video.**

**REAL STUDENT**

*Are you the same as Irene?*

# I'VE NEVER BEEN HAPPIER!

## 1 LANGUAGE IN CONTEXT

**A** Make a list of ten things you want to do in your life. Use the suggestions below, or think of other things.

| | | | |
|---|---|---|---|
| buy a car | learn to cook | move to a different city | travel to another country |
| buy an apartment | learn to drive | run a marathon | |
| find a new job | live in a different country | teach someone something | write a book |
| get married | | | write a song |
| have a baby | | | |

**B** Read about Elena and her grandmother, Maria. <u>Underline</u> the activities from exercise 1A that they talk about in the interview.

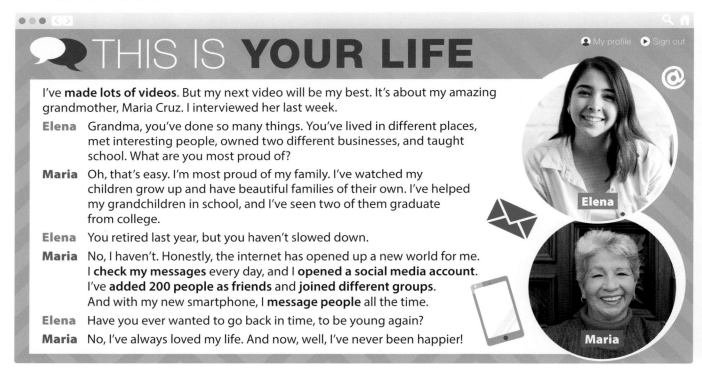

**THIS IS YOUR LIFE**

🔍 🏠

👤 My profile ▶ Sign out

I've **made lots of videos**. But my next video will be my best. It's about my amazing grandmother, Maria Cruz. I interviewed her last week.

**Elena** Grandma, you've done so many things. You've lived in different places, met interesting people, owned two different businesses, and taught school. What are you most proud of?

**Maria** Oh, that's easy. I'm most proud of my family. I've watched my children grow up and have beautiful families of their own. I've helped my grandchildren in school, and I've seen two of them graduate from college.

**Elena** You retired last year, but you haven't slowed down.

**Maria** No, I haven't. Honestly, the internet has opened up a new world for me. I **check my messages** every day, and I **opened a social media account**. I've **added 200 people as friends** and **joined different groups**. And with my new smartphone, I **message people** all the time.

**Elena** Have you ever wanted to go back in time, to be young again?

**Maria** No, I've always loved my life. And now, well, I've never been happier!

**C** Read the article again. Who (Elena, Maria, or both of them) … ?

1 is part of a social network
2 discovered a new world
3 made many videos before now
4 is very proud of her grandchildren

**D** **PAIR WORK** Who is the most interesting person you know? Tell your partner about the person.

## 2 VOCABULARY: Using verb–noun internet phrases

**A** 🔊 **2.36** Look at the words in **bold** in the text and complete the phrases below. Listen and check.

1 open _____
2 join _____
3 make _____
4 _____ someone
5 _____ someone as a friend
6 _____ your messages

B  🔊 **2.37** **Complete the verb–noun phrases using the words from the box. Listen and check. Were you right?**

| a website | left or right | on a link | your password |
|---|---|---|---|

7  build _____  9  click _____

8  change _____  10  swipe _____

C  ▶ **Now do the vocabulary exercises for 11.1 on page 151.**

D  PAIR WORK **Do your parents or grandparents use the internet. What do they do? What don't they do? Use the verb-noun phrases from exercise 2.**

> My grandfather checks his messages once a week. He doesn't want to open a social media account.

## 3  GRAMMAR: Present perfect for experience

A  **Circle the correct options to complete the rules. Use the sentences in the grammar box to help you. Underline other examples of the present perfect in the interview on page 108.**

1  To make the present perfect, use **have** / **make** + past participle.

2  For some verbs, the participle is the same as the **simple past** / **present** form.

3  The sentences are about experiences in the **present** / **general past**.

4  To ask if something has happened at any time in the past, use _____ .

5  To give a negative response, use _____ in your answer.

> **Present perfect for experience**
>
> I**'ve made** lots of videos.
> I**'ve added** 200 people as friends.
>
> **Have** you **ever wanted** to go back in time?
> I**'ve never been** happier!

B  ▶ **Now go to page 139. Look at the grammar chart and do the grammar exercise for 11.1.**

C  **Look at the list of activities in exercise 1A on page 108. Which have you done? Which haven't you done? Find the past participle of the verbs. Write five sentences that are true for you. Check your accuracy. Tell your partner. Have you done the same things?**

> I've learned to drive, but I haven't bought a car.

✓ **ACCURACY** CHECK

Use *never* + an affirmative verb.
Don't use *not* with *never*.

I've ~~not never~~ built a website. ✗
I've never built a website. ✓

## 4  SPEAKING

GROUP WORK **Write a questionnaire with the activities in exercise 1A on page 108. Ask your classmates the questions and write down who has done each thing. Who has done the most things? Who has done the things you want to do?**

> Have you run a marathon?

> Yes, I have.

> Great! What's your name?

# SOCIAL MEDIA LIKES

## 1 LANGUAGE IN CONTEXT

A   PAIR WORK   **Answer the questions with a partner.**

**A** Have you ever crowd-sourced information?

**B** Have you ever built an app?

**C** Have you ever made a video that went viral?

**D** Have you, or anyone you know, ever found love online?

B   ◀)) **2.38** **Listen to three people talk about their online experiences. Which three questions from exercise 1A does the interviewer ask?**

**1** Alex ☐       **2** Padma ☐       **3** Sara ☐

C   ◀)) **2.38**   PAIR WORK   **Listen again. Complete the second question the interviewer asks each person. Check your understanding with a partner.**

◀)) **2.38 Audio script**

**1**

**Alex**   Not viral really, but my friend and I **uploaded** a video that got about 7,500 views.

**Interviewer**   What _____?

**Alex**   Last year. It was about what music people have on their phones. A guy from the local newspaper even wrote an article about us.

**2**

**Padma**   I haven't, but my friend has.

**Interviewer**   What _____?

**Padma**   Well, my friend, Ananya, thought she found her cousin Rohan on Facebook. She added him as a friend, but he wasn't her cousin. Same name, different person. She messaged him about the mistake, and he messaged her back, and it continued. Then they decided to meet. They got married last year!

**3**

**Sara**   Yes, I have.

**Interviewer**   What _____?

**Sara**   We wanted to go to Florida on vacation, but didn't know where to go and what to do. So I put the question out there. I **follow** a photographer from Florida on Instagram, and she messaged me with lots of great travel tips: places to see, really good restaurants, that sort of thing. We got a lot of good suggestions from people, but her advice was the best.

D   **Read the answers again. Which person … ?**

**1** has a friend whose husband and cousin both have the same name   _____

**2** has been in the local newspaper   _____

**3** got travel advice from strangers online   _____

## 2 VOCABULARY: Using social media verbs

A  🔊 **2.39** **Match the internet icons with the words in the box. You can use your phone to help you. Listen and check.**

| block | bookmark | download | follow | go viral |
| like | log in | search for | share | upload |

B ➤ **Now do the vocabulary exercises for 11.2 on page 151.**

## 3 GRAMMAR: Present perfect and simple past

A **Circle the correct options to complete the rules. Use the questions in the grammar box to help you. Then find other examples of the present perfect and simple past in the text in exercise 1B on page 110.**

1 We use the **simple past / present perfect** to talk about past experiences <u>not</u> at a specific time.

2 We use the **simple past / present perfect** to talk about a specific time in the past.

> **Present perfect and simple past**
>
> **Have** you **ever made** a video that went viral?
> What **was** it about, and when **did** you **make** it?

B ➤ **Now go to page 139. Look at the grammar chart and do the grammar exercise for 11.2.**

C **PAIR WORK** **Write five present perfect sentences about yourself with these verbs. Then give details about each one with the simple past. Tell your partner. Have you done any of the same things?**

| eat | lose | break | read | see |

## 4 SPEAKING

A **GROUP WORK** **Ask your classmates the questions on the right. Make a note of their answers.**

B **Who has been online the most? Who is the biggest user of social media? For ideas, watch Allison's video.**

 REAL STUDENT *Did you go online as much as Allison today?*

### IN THE **LAST WEEK ... ?**

- How many times have you logged in to your social media account?
- How many people have you stopped following on social media?
- Tell me about one comment that you have posted.
- What's the most embarrassing thing you have shared on social media?
- Have you bookmarked anything?

# CAN I USE YOUR PHONE?

## 1 FUNCTIONAL LANGUAGE

A 🔊 **2.40** PAIR WORK **Look at the pictures. What has happened in picture A? What are the people doing in picture B? Read and listen to check.**

🔊 **2.40 Audio script**

**1** **A** Hello. Can I help you?

**B** Oh, hi … yes. **Would you mind** looking at my phone?

**A** **Sure**. What's the problem?

**B** I dropped it yesterday and broke the screen.

**A** I can see that!

**B** So, **can you** fix it?

**A** **I'm afraid not**. We don't fix screens here.

**B** Oh, I see. Thanks anyway.

**2** **A** This is so beautiful. Let's take a selfie.

**B** Smile! Oh, no!

**A** What's wrong?

**B** My phone. The battery's dead. **Do you mind if I** use yours?

**A** **No problem**.

**B** Thanks. OK … Smile! … Perfect. Actually, **could I** take a few more?

**A** **Yeah**, **that's fine**. I can share them with you later.

**B** Great. Thanks so much.

B **Complete the chart with expressions in bold from the conversations above.**

| Making requests | Responding to requests |
|---|---|
| **Asking someone to do something** | **Accepting** |
| Would you ¹_____ (looking at my phone)? | Sure. |
| ²_____ / Could you (fix it)? | No ⁵_____. |
| | Yeah, that's ⁶_____. |
| **Asking for permission** | **Refusing** |
| Do you mind ³_____ I (use your phone)? | I'm ⁷_____ not. |
| Can / ⁴_____ I (take a few more)? | No, I'm sorry. |

**INSIDER ENGLISH**

When a phone battery has no power, you can say that it's *dead*.
*The battery is **dead**.*
*My phone **died**.*

C PAIR WORK **Practice the conversations in exercise 1A with a partner.**

## 2 REAL-WORLD STRATEGY

A 🔊 **2.41** Listen to a conversation in a repair shop. What's the problem?

B 🔊 **2.41** Read the information in the box about remembering words. Then listen to the conversation again. What question from the box does the customer use?

> **REMEMBERING WORDS**
>
> When you can't remember a word, someone's name, or don't know how to say something in English, you can ask a question:
>
> *What's his/her name?*     *What do you call it/them?*

C 🔊 **2.42** Complete another conversation with a question from the box. Listen and check.

**A** I uploaded a photo of that actor I saw.

**B** Who?

**A** You know, _____? The really good one. She won an award last year.

**B** Oh, yeah. With all the hair. I know who you mean. What *is* her name?

D ▶ **Student A: Go to page 158. Student B: Go to page 160. Follow the instructions.**

## 3 PRONUNCIATION: Saying final /n/ and /m/ sounds

A 🔊 **2.43** Listen to the words. Focus on the sound of the **bold** letters. Practice saying them. Do you make the /n/ and /m/ sounds?

/n/ pho**n**e     broke**n**     wo**n**          /m/ proble**m**     progra**m**     na**m**e

B 🔊 **2.44** Circle the words that end in the /m/ sound. Listen and check. Practice the conversations with a partner. Is your mouth open or closed when you say the /m/ sound?

**1 A** What's the problem?
   **B** My phone is broken. Can you fix it?
   **A** I'm afraid not.

**2 A** What's his name?
   **B** It's Robin.

**3 A** It's warm in here.
   **B** The windows are closed.
   **A** Do you mind if I open them?
   **B** That's fine.

## 4 SPEAKING

PAIR WORK  **Choose two of the situations. Practice making and responding to requests. You can accept or refuse each request.**

**1** You're a tourist. Ask someone to take your picture.

**2** You're in an office or on a bus, and it's very hot. Check if it's OK to open the window.

**3** You're having a problem buying a soda from a machine. Another person is waiting.

**4** You're in a hurry to a buy a train ticket. You want to go to the front of the line.

*Would you mind taking a photo of us?*

*Sure. No problem.*

*Thanks a lot. Just press here.*

## 1 READING

**A** PAIR WORK How often do you take selfies? Find a selfie that you love or hate. Talk about where, when, and how you took the picture.

**B** READ FOR MAIN IDEAS Read the blog page. Check (✓) the topics that the writer includes.

1 how often people take selfies ☐
2 problems with selfies (selfie fails!) ☐
3 selfies and social media ☐
4 famous people's selfies ☐

5 the age of people who take selfies ☐
6 how to take a good selfie ☐
7 why people take selfies ☐
8 where people take selfies ☐

---

● ● ● ◉ ‹ ›     🔍 🏠

About | Blog | Images | Archive

 **Diana Garcia** @dgarcia

Thanks to all my friends (174!) who answered my questions about selfies. Here's the result – it's a mini-project for my Media and Communication course. I hope you like it – comments welcome!

♡ 36   💬 21   🔁 17

Posted 3:15 p.m.   + Comment

## SELFIES IN NUMBERS

### WHO'S TAKING SELFIES?

FEMALES **36%**  MALES **64%**

AGE
18   19%
19   65%
20   6%
21 and over   10%

### HOW WE SHARE

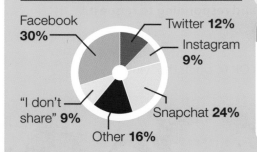

Facebook **30%**
Twitter **12%**
Instagram **9%**
Snapchat **24%**
"I don't share" **9%**
Other **16%**

### TOP SITUATIONS FOR SELFIES

**30%** at a party/on a night out
**34%** on vacation
**20%** at school
**16%** in front of the mirror
**30%** with a friend/a group of friends
**18%** with a boyfriend/girlfriend
**52%** alone

### CHANGING SELFIES

I have used an app to …

 … change my hair **37%**
 … add glasses or a silly mustache **32%**
 … add a special filter **25%**
 … change my eye color **6%**

### TOP REASONS FOR SELFIES

1 to remember a happy moment
2 because you feel good
3 because you look good
4 to share information about your life

**FUN FACT!!**
PEOPLE TAKE **TWO** SELFIES A DAY ON AVERAGE.

 ✓

---

**C** READ FOR DETAIL Read the blog again. Which sentences are true? Correct the false ones.

1 Teenagers take the most selfies.
2 Parties are the most popular place for selfies.
3 People take selfies with friends the most.
4 People often take selfies when they're happy.
5 Most people share their selfies on social media.
6 Apps are popular for changing eye color.

D **PAIR WORK** **THINK CRITICALLY** Choose the statement that best summarizes Diana's infographic about selfies. Discuss your ideas with a partner.

A People take them because they are lonely.

B They're about sharing positive experiences.

C They're not fashionable now.

D They're a good way to make friends.

## 2 WRITING

A **Look at the comments about Diana's infographic. Which are positive, and which are negative?**

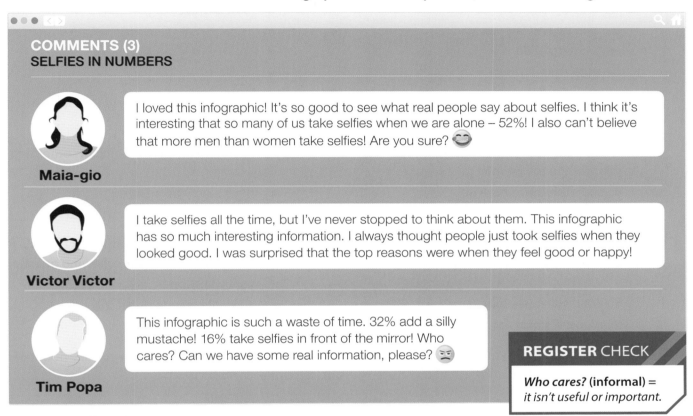

**COMMENTS (3)**
**SELFIES IN NUMBERS**

**Maia-gio**
I loved this infographic! It's so good to see what real people say about selfies. I think it's interesting that so many of us take selfies when we are alone – 52%! I also can't believe that more men than women take selfies! Are you sure? 😂

**Victor Victor**
I take selfies all the time, but I've never stopped to think about them. This infographic has so much interesting information. I always thought people just took selfies when they looked good. I was surprised that the top reasons were when they feel good or happy!

**Tim Popa**
This infographic is such a waste of time. 32% add a silly mustache! 16% take selfies in front of the mirror! Who cares? Can we have some real information, please? 😠

**REGISTER** CHECK

*Who cares?* (informal) = *it isn't useful or important.*

B **WRITING SKILLS** Look at the phrases in the box. Match them to their uses. Find more examples in the comments in exercise A.

| I always thought … | I think it's interesting that … | Who cares? |

1 to say something positive: _____

2 to say something negative: _____

3 to say that you had a different idea before: _____

C **PAIR WORK** Look at the infographic on page 114 again. Which information do you think is most interesting? Which information is <u>not</u> interesting? Why?

 **WRITE IT**

D **Use your answers in exercise 2C to help you write a short comment of about 50 words. You can:**

  ■ say what you like or don't like about the infographic

  ■ ask a question about the information

  ■ use emojis, like these: 😄 😠

E **PAIR WORK** Show your comment to a partner. Write a reply to your partner's comment.

# TIME TO SPEAK
## Online videos

**A** **Look at the types of videos on sites like YouTube. Which ones have you watched? Do you know any others? Add them to the list.**

- music videos
- beauty and fashion advice
- "how-to" videos
- cute animal videos

- food or travel vlogs
- _____
- _____
- _____

**B** **RESEARCH** **Think of a famous YouTuber. What do they make videos about? Can you describe them to the class? Why do you think they are popular?**

**C** **DISCUSS** **Imagine you're going to make a video. What is it going to be about? Think of something you want to tell people, for example:**

- something you have done
- somewhere you have been

- something you are interested in
- something you know how to do

**D** **PREPARE** **In small groups, you are going to make a video. Plan what you are going to say and do in the video. Use the phrases at the bottom of the page to help you. Think about the following questions:**

- What type of video will you make?
- What will it be about?
- Who will star in your video? What will they say?

- What will happen in your video?
- Who will film and direct the video?

 **E** **PRESENT** **Show your video to your classmates, and watch their videos. What do you like about each video? Do you think there are any future YouTube celebrities in your class?**

*To check your progress, go to page 156.*

# USEFUL PHRASES

**DISCUSS**
Have you heard of … ?
I really like watching his/her/
their videos because …

**PREPARE**
I have a good idea.
I think we should …
How about … ?

**PRESENT**
This is our video.
That's really cool/funny/interesting.
You've done a really good job!
I think you'll be famous one day!

- talk about the weather
- describe places, people, and things
- ask for and give directions
- write simple instructions
- create a tourism campaign for your country

# OUTDOORS

## 12

## START SPEAKING

A  Look at the picture. What's happening? What time of year do you think it is? Why? Think of <u>three</u> causes for wildfires like this one.

B  Do you ever have big fires in your country? Where and when do they usually happen? Have you ever seen a big fire?

C  Does it get very hot or very cold in your country? Which do you prefer, hot weather or cold weather? Why? For ideas, watch Allison's video.

**REAL STUDENT**

*Do you agree with Allison?*

# NINE MONTHS, EIGHT COUNTRIES

## 1  VOCABULARY: Describing weather

| DARK / WET | COLD | HOT | STORMY | EXTREME |
|---|---|---|---|---|
| cloudy | freezing | boiling | blizzard | drought |
| foggy | snowy | sunny | snowstorm | flood |
| humid | | | thunder and lightning | hurricane |
| rainy | | | windy | |

A  🔊 2.45  Listen and repeat the weather words. Can you think of more words for each category?

B  Look at the list of weather words again. Which are adjectives? Underline them. Which are nouns? Circle them.

C  ▶ Now do the vocabulary exercises for 12.1 on page 152.

D  PAIR WORK  How would you describe your local weather for different seasons?

> **!** For temperatures, we use "degrees."
> 24° C = 24 *degrees* Celsius
> 65° F = 65 *degrees* Fahrenheit

## 2  LANGUAGE IN CONTEXT

A  🔊 2.46  Listen to the introduction to a radio interview. Who is Jonathan Brookner? Why is he in the studio?

B  🔊 2.47  Think of three questions you want to ask Jonathan about his trip. Then listen to the interview. Did the interviewer ask the same questions?

### 🔊 2.47 Audio script

**Host** Jonathan, tell us some more about your adventures. What was the weather like in all these places?

**Jonathan** We experienced every kind of weather possible! In Patagonia, we were in a **snowstorm** that lasted for three days. It was **freezing** and so **windy**!

**Host** That's a long time to be in the middle of a snowstorm!

**Jonathan** In Ecuador it was worse! There was a huge tropical storm, with really heavy rain and **thunder and lightning**. There were **floods**, and the roads were closed. We stayed there for a few days to help the local people clean up the mess.

**Host** Did you get any good weather?

**Jonathan** Uruguay had good weather. It was perfect: warm and **sunny**.

**Host** Thanks Jonathan, let's take another short break, we'll be back in two minutes …

C ◀)) **2.47** **Read and listen again. Answer the questions.**

1  What weather did Jonathan enjoy most?

2  What weather did he enjoy least?

3  What extreme weather did they experience?

D  PAIR WORK  **What's your favorite kind of weather? What is your least favorite kind of weather? Why? Where and when have you experienced each of them?**

## 3 GRAMMAR: *be like*

A  **Complete the rules. Use the sentences in the grammar box to help you.**

1  Use the verb _____ + *like* to ask questions about things.

2  Answer these questions with **verbs** / **adjectives**.

> **be like**
>
> What **was** the weather **like**?
> It **was** freezing and so windy.

B  **Draw lines to match the questions (1–3) and answers (a–c).**

1  What's the weather like?

2  What was the party like?

3  What will the course be like?

a  It'll be hard work!

b  It's cold and windy.

c  It was great! We had a really good time.

C  ▶  **Now go to page 140. Look at the grammar chart and do the grammar exercise for 12.1.**

D  PAIR WORK  **Think about a person you've known for a long time. Ask and answer the questions. Check your accuracy. Then tell your partner.**

1  What was he/she like when he/she was younger?

2  Is he/she very different now? What is he/she like today?

> ✓ **ACCURACY** CHECK
>
> **When you are answering a question with *what … like?* don't use *like* with adjectives in the answer.**
> *What was the weather like?*
> It was ~~like~~ cold and windy. ✗
> It was cold and windy. ✓

## 4 SPEAKING

A  GROUP WORK  **Think of a city you know well. Answer the questions.**

■  What's the weather like in your city today? What's it going to be like next weekend?

■  What's the weather usually like in December? In July?

■  Does the city have good weather in general?

B  **Tell the class your answers to the questions in exercise 4A with more details.**

# THIS TRIP HAS IT ALL

## 1 VOCABULARY: Describing landscapes and cityscapes

A Look at the pictures. What do you think the weather is like in each place? Which picture do you like the most? Why?

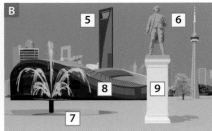

B 🔊 2.48 Which features from the box can you usually find in the city? In nature? Listen and repeat. Then label the pictures with what you can see.

| | | | | |
|---|---|---|---|---|
| ☐ cave | ☐ cliff | ☐ coast | ☐ fountain | ☐ glacier |
| 1 rainforest | ☐ rocks | ☐ skyscraper | ☐ stadium | ☐ statue |
| ☐ stream | ☐ tower | ☐ valley | ☐ waterfall | |

C ▶ Now do the vocabulary exercises for 12.2 on page 152.

D PAIR WORK Think of the landscape around your town. What's it like? Which landscape features can you find near you? Which cityscape features can you find near you?

## 2 LANGUAGE IN CONTEXT

A PAIR WORK When you travel, do you prefer to go to the coast, the mountains, or the city? Why?

B Read about a trip to Ecuador. Would you like to take this trip?

### EIGHT DAYS IN ECUADOR
Day by day   Dates and prices   Accommodation

From the skyscrapers of Quito to the rocky cliffs of the Galapagos Islands, this trip has it all! Everyone who takes this trip falls in love with our beautiful country.

**DAY 1**
You'll take a guided tour around Quito. We have tour guides that speak English and Spanish. If you'd like a tour in another language, just ask! The tour will end at the top of El Panecillo Hill, where you can see the famous Virgen de Quito **statue** and take photos of the amazing views of the city and the mountains all around it.

**DAY 2**
You will leave the busy city and take a plane to Baltra in the Galapagos Islands. You'll get on a boat which goes to the Charles Darwin Research Station. You can learn about the strange animals that live on the islands and the interesting trees and flowers that grow there. You can even see some of the giant tortoises walking around on the **rocks**.

**DAY 3**
. . .

C Read the information again. What can you do in Quito? What can you do in the Galapagos Islands?

D  PAIR WORK  Are there different landscapes in your
country? How many different kinds can you name?
Describe them. Which one do you like the most? Why?
For ideas, watch Seung Geyoung's video.

**REAL STUDENT**

*Is your favorite place like Seung Geyoung's?*

## 3 GRAMMAR: Relative pronouns: *who, which, that*

A  (Circle) the correct options to complete the rules. Use the sentences in the grammar box to help you.

1  Use *who/which* and *that* for people.
2  Use *who/which* and *that* for things.

> **Relative pronouns: *who, which, that***
>
> Everyone **who** takes this trip falls in love with our beautiful country.
> We have our tour guides **that** speak English and Spanish.
> You'll get on a boat **which** goes to the Charles Darwin Research Station.
> You can learn about the strange animals **that** live there.

B  ▶ **Now go to page 140. Look at the grammar chart and do the grammar exercise for 12.2 .**

> **!** You can use *that* for both people and things.
>
> *That's the man **that** we met in Quito. Remember? He's wearing the hat **that** he bought at the market there.*

## 4 SPEAKING

A  **Complete the descriptions using *who*, *which*, or *that*.
Then think of a person, object, or place for each of the descriptions.**

1  the person _____ helped me most at school
2  a song _____ reminds me of summer
3  a landscape _____ makes me feel relaxed
4  the people _____ I spend the most time with
5  one thing _____ I would really like to do in the future

B  PAIR WORK  **Tell your partner about your answers in exercise 4A.**

# 12.3 I THINK WE'RE LOST

## 1 FUNCTIONAL LANGUAGE

A 🔊 **2.49** **Have you ever gotten lost? Where were you? Did you ask for help? Read and listen to the conversations. Where do the people want to go?**

🔊 **2.49 Audio script**

1  A  Hello, **excuse me, we're looking for the waterfall. Are we going in the right direction?**

   B  The waterfall? No, **you need to go back the way you came.**

   A  Oh. That's a long way.

   B  See that hill there?

   A  The one with the tall tree on top?

   B  Yes, **turn right after that hill. Walk for a couple of miles, and you'll see the waterfall on the left.**

   A  Thanks. I hope this is a really beautiful waterfall.

2  A  **Excuse me, can you help us, please? We're lost,** and my phone just died.

   B  Yeah, sure. Where do you want to go?

   A  Well, **we need to get to** the nearest subway station.

   B  OK, let me look at my phone … . Yeah, **at the next intersection turn right. Walk three blocks** to King Street **and then turn left.** You'll see the park ahead of you. **The subway station's right there.**

   A  That's great. Thanks!

   B  Keep walking toward the park and you can't miss it!

### INSIDER ENGLISH

People often say *you can't miss it* when a place is really easy to find.

B  **Complete the chart with expressions in bold from the conversations above.**

| Asking for directions | Giving directions |
|---|---|
| Excuse me, we're <sup>1</sup> _____ for (the waterfall).<br><br>Are we going in the <sup>2</sup> _____ direction?<br><br>Excuse me, <sup>3</sup> _____<br><br>_____ us, please? We're <sup>4</sup> _____ . | You need to <sup>5</sup> _____ the way you came. <sup>6</sup> _____ right (after the hill). Walk for (a couple of miles), and you'll see (the waterfall) <sup>7</sup> _____ .<br><br>At the next intersection <sup>8</sup> _____ right. Walk (three) <sup>9</sup> _____ and then turn left. The (subway station's) right <sup>10</sup> _____ . |

C  **PAIR WORK** **Practice the conversations in exercise 1A with your partner.**

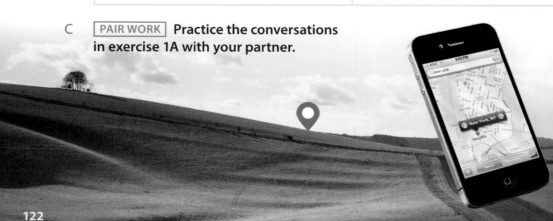

## 2 REAL-WORLD STRATEGY

A  🔊 **2.50** Listen to the conversation. Where does the woman want to go?

B  🔊 **2.50** Read the information about correcting yourself in the box below. Listen to the conversation again. How many times does the man correct himself with the phrases from the box?

> **CORRECTING YOURSELF**
>
> When you've given incorrect information, you can correct yourself with these phrases:
>
> *Well, actually …*      *No, wait …*

C  PAIR WORK  Write <u>three</u> sentences about you. Give a <u>wrong</u> detail in each sentence. Then tell a partner your sentence, and correct the information.

## 3 PRONUNCIATION: Saying /w/ at the beginning of a word

A  🔊 **2.51** Listen. Focus on the sound of the letters in **bold**. Practice saying them. Do you make the /w/ sound?

Excuse me, **w**e're looking for the **w**aterfall.

B  🔊 **2.52** Listen. Which speaker, A or B, says the /w/ sound?

A  **W**here are you and your **w**ife **w**alking to?

B  **W**e're **w**alking to the **w**aterfall.

A  **W**ait, this isn't the **w**ay to the **w**aterfall!

B  **W**ell, actually, we **w**ant to **w**alk through the **w**oods first because the **w**eather's so **w**indy.

C  PAIR WORK  Practice the conversation in exercise 3B. Focus on the /w/ sounds. Look at the conversations in exercise 1A on page 122. Find more examples of words with the /w/ sound at the beginning.

## 4 SPEAKING

A  PAIR WORK  Think about special places in your town. Take turns asking for and giving directions to those places from where you are now. Remember to check that you understand the directions. You can use the map on your phone.

B  Were your directions accurate, or did you have to correct yourself? Whose directions were the easiest to follow?

# 12.4 GUERRILLA GARDENING

## 1 LISTENING

A **PREDICT** Look at the pictures. Where are the people? What are they doing? Why do you think they're doing it at night?

B 🔊 **2.53** **LISTEN FOR SPECIFIC INFORMATION** Listen to Bruna Andreotti talking about guerrilla gardening. Check your predictions in exercise 1A.

C 🔊 **2.53** **LISTEN FOR DETAILS** Listen again. Complete the sentences.

1 A guerrilla gardener is a person who _____ .
2 They plant things on land that _____ .
3 They do it to make their neighborhoods _____ .
4 Bruna's group runs a community garden that _____ .

D **PAIR WORK** **THINK CRITICALLY** Do you think guerrilla gardens are a good idea for improving city neighborhoods? Why or why not? What other solutions are there?

E Which places would be good for a guerrilla gardening project in your city? Would you like to be part of a project like this? Why or why not?

## 2 PRONUNCIATION: Listening for *t* when it sounds like *d*

A 🔊 **2.54** Listen. Focus on the **bold** letters. What letter do they sound like?

1 in the middle of a ci**t**y
2 People throw less li**tt**er.
3 They si**t** outside on the street.

B 🔊 **2.55** (Circle) the letter *t* when it changes to sound like *d*. What sounds are before and after it? Listen and check.

1 a really positive effect
2 We also have a community garden.
3 It's about working together to do something good for our city and our community.

C **Complete the sentence.**

The letter *t* is often pronounced like ___ when it is between two _____ sounds.

## 3 WRITING

**A** Read these instructions for how to be a guerrilla gardener. Would you add any steps?

HOW TO ...
**be a guerrilla gardener**

Here are **five simple steps** to get started as a guerrilla gardener. *Anyone can do it!*

First, choose a place in your neighborhood that nobody uses or cares about.

Then, decide what kinds of plants you want to plant. Flowers? Fruit? Vegetables?

Next, go to a gardening center and choose your plants. Also, buy any tools you might need.

Now go out at a quiet time and plant your plants.

Finally, water your plants and watch them grow!

**B** **WRITING SKILLS** Read the text again and find the sequence words in the box. Complete the sentences below.

| finally | first | next | now | then |
| --- | --- | --- | --- | --- |

1 Use _____ to introduce the starting point.

2 Use _____, _____, and _____ to show the order of other points.

3 Use _____ to make the last point.

**C** You're going to write a short how-to text like the one in exercise 3A. Decide what you're going to write about. Use one of the ideas here or your own idea.

*Five simple steps to ...*
- making spaghetti
- dancing salsa
- choosing a pet
- learning new vocabulary

**WRITE IT**

**D** Decide on the five steps. Read the text in exercise 3A again and <u>underline</u> any phrases you can use. Then write your text. Keep your text short and simple, and remember to use sequence words.

**E** **PAIR WORK** Read some of your classmates' texts. Which are the easiest instructions to follow? Can you remember the instructions? Tell your partner.

# TIME TO SPEAK
## Places that you'll love

**A** **DISCUSS** Look at the three pictures. What can you see in each one? Which place would you most like to visit? Why? Are there similar places near you?

Tofino Beach

Lake Monroe

The Rockies

**B** All three pictures are from the same country. What country do you think it is? Why?

**C** Read the announcement. Discuss the questions to help think of ideas for your entry.

- What different kinds of landscapes are in your country? Make a list of places that are very interesting and/or beautiful.
- Which places in your country are famous? Why are they famous?
- Which places are the most popular with visitors? Are there any special places that most tourists don't know about? Where are they? Why are they special?
- What's the weather like in different seasons? When is the best time of year to visit?

**D** **PREPARE** Work with a partner and prepare an entry for your country. Use the phrases at the bottom of the page to help you.

- Choose three places which you think tourists would like. What are they like? What can you do there?
- Write your reasons for choosing each place.
- Think of at least one slogan for the tourism campaign.
- Write a description of the three photos you want to include with your entry. Go online to find some examples if you want.

FIND IT

**E** **PRESENT** Present your entry to the class. Listen to the other presentations, and decide which places you want to go to and why. Which campaign had the best slogan?

To check your progress, go to page 156.

## COME TO OUR COUNTRY!

The Tourism Office needs your help with a program to attract tourists to our beautiful country.

**PLACES:** Send us information about three spectacular places in our country that you think should be on our tourism site. Explain why you think each one is special, and suggest photos for each of the three places.

**SLOGANS:** Send us your ideas for a phrase or sentence to get people's attention and make them want to know more about our country.

Submissions are due by *September 21*.

# USEFUL PHRASES

**DISCUSS**
I'd really like to go there because …
It looks exciting / pretty / amazing.
It's similar to where I live.

**PREPARE**
Where do you want to talk about?
Have you ever been to … ? / Do you know … well?

**PRESENT**
We think tourists would love … because …
This place is really special to me because …

# REVIEW 4 (UNITS 10–12)

## 1 VOCABULARY

A **Put the words in the box into the correct categories.**

| | | | | | | |
|---|---|---|---|---|---|---|
| accountant | ankle | architect | block | cliff | coast | fever |
| follow | freezing | humid | hurricane | mechanic | neck | nurse |
| search | share | stomachache | stream | thunder | valley | waterfall |

Jobs: _____

Health and body: _____

The internet: _____

Weather: _____

Landscapes: _____

B **PAIR WORK** **Think of one more word from each category. Add them to the lists in exercise 1A. Compare with a partner. Did you write the same words?**

## 2 GRAMMAR

A **Circle the correct options to complete the conversations.**

1 **A** You ¹*'ve been / went* to a glacier, haven't you? What ²*are they / was it* like?

  **B** Yes, I ³*have / am*. It was freezing!

2 **A** How do I block these ads ⁴*that / who* appear on my screen all the time?

  **B** It's easy. You ⁵*don't have to / have to* download anything. Just click there.

3 **A** What's the weather ⁶*going to be like / going to like* at the coast?

  **B** A friend ⁷*has told / told* me yesterday that it ⁸*might be / might being* rainy.

B **PAIR WORK** **Complete the sentences so that they are true for you. Compare them with a partner.**

1 I've never been to … .

  *I've never been to Europe, but I'd love to go one day.*

2 I have a friend who … .

3 Every week I have to … .

4 Tomorrow morning I think I might … .

5 Last week I bought something that … .

## 3 SPEAKING

A **PAIR WORK** **Think of a beautiful place in your country that you have been to. Follow the instructions for the conversation.**

1 Ask your partner if he/she has ever been to that place.

2 Exchange opinions using questions with *what … like*.

3 Talk about the best things that people can see or do there.

4 Invite your partner to come to that place with you sometime soon. Use *have to* and *don't have to* to encourage your partner to come.

## 4 FUNCTIONAL LANGUAGE

A Complete the conversation at a basketball game.

> can I    could you    hurts    no problem    sure    what happened?    you mind

A Are you OK? ¹_____

B I twisted my ankle. It really ²_____ .

A How ³_____ help?

B ⁴_____ get a chair for me, please? And maybe some ice?

A ⁵_____ , just a second … Here you go. Do you think we should call an ambulance?

B No, I don't think that's necessary. But would ⁶_____ getting me a taxi?

A ⁷_____ . I'll call for one right now.

B Thank you!

B PAIR WORK Practice reading the conversation in pairs.

C Read the directions. Where do you get to from where you are now?

1 Turn left as you go out of the door. At the next intersection, turn right. Walk for three blocks.

2 Turn right at the door. Walk for four blocks. Cross the street and take the first left.

D Where is the nearest grocery store? Write down some more directions and read them to your partner. Were your directions the same as your partner's?

## 5 SPEAKING

A PAIR WORK Choose one of the situations. Act it out in pairs.

1 You have a bad toothache. Go to the drugstore. Explain your problem and ask for advice.

A Hello, can I help you?

B Yes, please. I have a horrible toothache …

2 You have broken the screen on your phone. Go to a phone shop and ask them to replace the screen. Ask about the price and the time it will take.

A Hello, can you help me?

B I can try. What's the problem?

3 Some tourists stop you outside the school. They are lost. They want directions to the nearest subway or bus stop. Help them.

A Excuse me, can you help us? We're lost.

B Sure. Where do you want to go?

B Change roles and repeat the role play.

# GRAMMAR REFERENCE AND PRACTICE

## 7.1 QUANTIFIERS (page 67)

| Count nouns … | Non-count nouns … |
|---|---|
| have a singular and plural form. <br> chili    chilies | do not have a plural form. <br> ~~rices~~    rice |
| use *a/an* for the singular. <br> a chili | do not use *a/an*. <br> ~~a rice~~    rice |
| use *some* with plural nouns in affirmative sentences. <br> I'd like **some** chilies. | use *some* in affirmative sentences. <br> I ate **some** rice. |
| use *any* in negative sentences and questions. <br> Do you have **any** chilies? <br> I don't have **any** chilies. | I didn't eat **any** rice. <br> Did you eat **any** rice? |

A  Circle the correct words to complete the sentences.

1  I eat *a few / a little* chocolate every day.
2  I don't have *many / much* time to cook.
3  I try to eat *some / too much* fruits and vegetables every day.
4  I like *some / a little* spicy dishes, but I don't eat them every day.
5  Too *much / many* sweet things are bad for you.
6  I know how to cook *a lot of / not many* dishes because I love cooking.

B  **Are the sentences in exercise A true for you? If not, change them to make them true for you.**

## 7.2 VERB PATTERNS (page 69)

| verb + *to* + verb | verb + verb + *-ing* |
|---|---|
| I **prefer to eat** at food trucks. | I usually **can't stand waiting** in line. |
| I **love to try** new food. | I **don't mind waiting** here. |

A  **Complete the sentences with the correct form of the verb in parentheses.**

1  My brother can't stand _____ (be) in the kitchen because he doesn't like the smell of cooking.
2  I'm going to go to the beach next month, so I want _____ (lose) some weight before then.
3  We love to cook together, so we hope _____ (open) a restaurant someday!
4  I don't enjoy _____ (cook) because it takes a lot of time.
5  Don't forget _____ (give) me your recipe – dinner was delicious.

## 8.1 *IF* AND *WHEN* (page 77)

| Statements |
|---|
| I always stay in a hotel near the airport **when** I travel for work. |
| **If** I want to explore the city, I use a good online guidebook. |
| **Questions** |
| **When** you travel, do you usually go by plane or by train? |
| Do you take a taxi **if** you're late for work? |

> **!** You can put *if/when* at the beginning or in the middle of a sentence, and the meaning doesn't change.
>
> *If I'm late for work, I take a taxi. = I take a taxi if I'm late for work.*
>
> You can use **when** for *if* and the meaning doesn't change.
>
> *When I'm late for work, I take a taxi. = I take a taxi **when** I'm late for work.*

A **Rewrite the sentences with *if* or *when* in the correct place.**

1 I'm on vacation, I love to go to the beach. (when)

   When I'm on vacation, I love to go to the beach.

2 We often go to the park the weather is nice. (if)

3 I'm always nervous I travel by plane. (when)

4 I can, I always prefer to stay in a modern hotel. (if)


## 8.2 GIVING REASONS USING *TO* AND *FOR* (page 79)

| Giving reasons using *to* and *for* |
|---|
| *to* + **verb** |
| to have lunch        to take a shower        to catch a bus |
| *for* + **noun** |
| **for** lunch        **for** the experience        **for** a shower |
| So, João, why are you going to Lima? |
| **To visit** Cuzco. And **for the experience**. It's an amazing trip! |

A **Write *to* or *for* to complete the sentences.**

1 Next weekend I'm going to Lima _____ a job interview.

2 Last week I visited my grandmother _____ interview her for a school project.

3 Tomorrow I'm going shopping _____ some new clothes.

4 I'm meeting my best friend later today _____ talk about our vacation plans.

5 I'm going to the library _____ study. It's too noisy at home!

6 My parents never come to my house _____ special events and celebrations. I always go there.

## 9.1 COMPARATIVE ADJECTIVES (page 87)

| Comparative adjectives | |
|---|---|
| short adjectives: add *-er* | cold → cold**er** (than)<br>wet → wet**ter** (than) |
| adjectives ending in -y: *-y* → *-i*, add *-er* | friendl**y** → friendl**ier** (than) |
| long adjectives: *more* or *less* + adjective | important → **more** important (than) → **less** important (than) |
| irregular adjectives | good → **better**<br>bad → **worse** |

A   **Use the words to write sentences. Use the comparative form of the adjectives.**

1   She / be / happy / in her new job / in her old one.   *She's happier in her new job than in her old one.*

2   She / have / interesting / earrings / me.

3   Your new scarf / be / nice / your old one.

4   I need a belt / that / be / big / this.

5   Your shoes / be / dirty / your shirt.

6   He is / tall / his father / now!

## 9.2 SUPERLATIVE ADJECTIVES (page 89)

| Superlative adjectives | |
|---|---|
| short adjectives: add *-est* | young → the young**est** |
| adjectives ending in -y: *-y* → *-i*, add *-est* | funny → the funn**iest** |
| long adjectives: *most* + adjective | important → the **most** important |
| irregular adjectives | good → the **best**<br>bad → the **worst** |

A   **Complete these fun facts with the superlative form of the adjectives in parentheses.**

1   The world's _____ (long) mustache is more than four meters long.

2   There is an international competition for the world's _____ (good) beard and mustache.

3   The _____ (big) hole in a pierced ear is 127 millimeters wide.

4   The _____ (expensive) earrings in the world cost $57.4 million.

5   An Indian man holds the world record for pulling the _____ (heavy) things with his beard.

## 10.1 *HAVE TO* (page 99)

| *have to* + verb | | | | |
|---|---|---|---|---|
| | **Affirmative** | **Negative** | **Question** | **Short answers** |
| I / You / We / They | **have to clean** the desks. | **don't have to eat** in the lunchroom. | **Do** you **have to eat** at your desk? | Yes, you **do**.<br>No, you **don't**. |
| He / She / It | **has to be** very clear. | **doesn't have to stay** outside. | **Does** it **have to be** so loud in here? | Yes, it **does**.<br>No, it **doesn't**. |

A  **Complete the sentences with the correct form of *have to* or a short answer.**

1  **A**  How many classes _____*do you have to go*_____ (you go) to each week?

   **B**  I _____ (go) to my English class three times a week.

2  **A**  _____ (you work) in the evenings or on weekends?

   **B**  No, we _____ . But sometimes we _____ (study) for tests then.

3  **A**  _____ (you give) your homework to your teacher online?

   **B**  No, I _____ . But I _____ (hand it in) on time!

4  **A**  _____ (your teacher correct) all your work?

   **B**  Yes, she _____ . She _____ (do) a lot of work outside of class.

## 10.2 MAKING PREDICTIONS (page 101)

| Making predictions | | | | |
|---|---|---|---|---|
| | **Affirmative** | **Negative** | **Question** | **Short answers** |
| I / He / She / It / You / We / They | **will / 'll<br>might     catch** a cold.<br>**may** | **will not / won't catch** a cold. | **Will** you **be** OK? | Yes, I **will**.<br>No, I **won't**. |

A  **Write the words in the correct order to make sentences.**

1  **A**  college / finish / soon / you / Will

   _____ ?

   **B**  finish / I / might / this / year

   _____ .

2  **A**  after / do / graduate / What / will / you / you

   _____ ?

   **B**  an / become / engineer / I / 'll / probably

   _____ .

3  **A**  boyfriend / get / married / to / Will / you / your

   _____ ?

   **B**  get / 'll / married / Maybe / in a few years / we

   _____ .

4  **A**  do / 'll / retire / think / When / you / you

   _____ ?

   **B**  be / before / I'm / won't / 65 / It

   _____ .

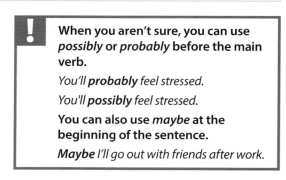

! When you aren't sure, you can use *possibly* or *probably* before the main verb.

*You'll* **probably** *feel stressed.*

*You'll* **possibly** *feel stressed.*

**You can also use** *maybe* **at the beginning of the sentence.**

**Maybe** *I'll go out with friends after work.*

# 11.1 PRESENT PREFECT FOR EXPERIENCE (page 109)

## Present perfect

We use the present perfect to talk about experiences.

We form the present perfect with *have/has* + past participle.

For regular verbs, the past participle looks the same as the simple past (played, called). See the inside of the back cover for a list of irregular verbs.

| | Affirmative | Negative | Question | Short answers |
|---|---|---|---|---|
| I / You / We / They | **have/'ve changed** my password. | **haven't changed** my password. | **Have** you (ever) **joined** a group. | Yes, I **have.** <br> No, we **haven't.** |
| He / She / It | **has/'s joined** a group. | **hasn't changed** his password. | **Has** it (ever) **snowed** in July? | Yes, it **has.** <br> No, it **hasn't.** |

A   **Complete the conversations in the present perfect.**

1  A  I ¹_____ never _____ (add) anyone as a friend on social media, but 200 people ²_____ (add) me. ³_____ you ever _____ (add) someone as a friend?

   B  No, I ⁴_____ , because I ⁵_____ never _____ (open) a social media account.

2  A  ⁶_____ you ever _____ (build) a website?

   B  Yes, I ⁷_____ . I ⁸_____ (build) three websites!

3  A  I ⁹_____ never _____ (change) my password.

   B  That's dangerous!

> ❗ **ever** = *any time up to now*
> *Have you* **ever** *seen snow?*
> **never** = *not ever*
> *I've* **never** *been to Peru.*

# 11.2 PRESENT PERFECT AND SIMPLE PAST (page 111)

## Present perfect and simple past

Use the present perfect to talk about past experiences when you don't specify when they happened. Use the simple past to say exactly when something happened.

| Questions | Answers |
|---|---|
| Have you ever been to China. | Yes, I have. |
| When did you go there? | I went last year. |
| I've never posted a video on social media. Have you? | Oh, yes. I've posted videos lots of times. |

A   **Read the sentences and write the present perfect or simple past of the verb in parentheses.**

1  A  This morning, I _____ (make) a video of myself singing. I want to upload it to my social media page, but I _____ (never do) that before. Can you help me?

   B  Ask Ryan. He _____ (upload) lots of videos. I _____ (never make) a video before.

2  A  _____ (ever feel) lonely when you're at school, far away from your family?

   B  Sure. I really _____ (miss) my mom yesterday, so I _____ (call) her.

3  A  I'm going to eat at Marcella's downtown tonight.

   B  Really? _____ (see) the prices on their menu?

   A  No. I _____ (go) online yesterday and _____ (search) for nice local restaurants. _____ (you eat) there before?

   B  No, never. It's really expensive.

## 12.1 QUESTIONS WITH *BE LIKE* (page 119)

| Questions with *be like* | | |
|---|---|---|
| Use questions with *what* + *be* + noun + *like* to ask for a description of something. | | |
| Simple present | What**'s** the weather **like**? | It's cold and windy. |
| Simple past | **What was** the party **like**? | It was great! |
| Future | **What will** the course **be like**? | It'll be hard work! |

A   **Write the words in the correct order to make questions.**

1   like / was / what / the / music / ?

2   what / like / new / 's / their / house / ?

3   was / father / what / his / like / ?

4   food / the / like / be / what / will / ?

5   the / like / was / movie / what / ?

6   will / like / test / the / be / what / ?

## 12.2 RELATIVE PRONOUNS: *WHO, WHICH, THAT* (page 121)

| Relative pronouns: *who, which, that* |
|---|
| Use *who*, *which*, and *that* to introduce new information about a person or object. |
| Use *who* and *that* for people.    I know the people **who** live there.    I know the people **that** live there. |
| Use *which* and *that* for things.    I like the plants **that** grow there.    I like the plants **which** grow there. |

A   **Combine the two sentences using *who, which,* or *that*. Make any other changes that are needed.**

1   I live in an apartment. My apartment is near the park.

I live in an apartment that is near the park.

2   There are mountains in the north. They have snow on them all year.

3   He works at the ski school. It is in the mountains near here.

4   Those are my neighbors. They live in the house next door to us.

5   This is the house on the coast. We rented it last year.

6   These are my friends from college. They came with us to the concert.

# VOCABULARY PRACTICE

## 7.1 NAMING FOOD (page 66)

A **Complete the text with the words in the box.**

| | | | |
|---|---|---|---|
| avocado | ~~cereal~~ | jam | lettuce |
| peanut butter | salmon | strawberries | yogurt |

**My daily food diary**

**Saturday**

A bowl of [1] ___cereal___ for **breakfast**, I just love granola!

**Lunch** with friends, a salad with [2] _____ and [3] _____ , and fruit for dessert: some fresh [4] _____ . Delicious!

At home, I make toast with [5] _____ and [6] _____ for the kids. They love that **snack** combination!

For dinner, we have [7] _____ with green vegetables. It's good to eat fish once a week. Then [8] _____ with honey for dessert – simple but healthy.

B **Circle the correct word to complete the sentences.**

1 I like *yogurt / chili* without sugar for breakfast.
2 I'm vegetarian, so I don't eat *burgers / avocados*.
3 I like a lot of *yogurt / onions* on my pizza.
4 I make corn with just butter, *salt / strawberries,* and pepper. Very simple, but very good.
5 Some people like bread with butter for breakfast, but many people like to put *cereal / jam* on it, too.

## 7.2 DESCRIBING FOOD (page 68)

A **Match the two parts to make a complete idea.**

1 Doctors say that raw vegetables are … ____    a I think it needs some sugar.
2 This chocolate is delicious! ____    b Can I have another piece, please?
3 That coffee is very bitter. ____    c good for your body.
4 I live by the sea … ____    d so we always have a lot of fresh fish to eat.
5 My favorite food isn't very healthy. ____    e It's a fried peanut butter sandwich with jam on top!
6 Thailand, Mexico, and India … ____    f are famous for their spicy food!

B **Complete the sentences from the conversations with the food words in the box.**

| | | | | | | | |
|---|---|---|---|---|---|---|---|
| boiled | delicious | fried | grilled | raw | roasted | sour | spicy |

1 If you have a bad stomach, don't eat too much [1] _____ food like curry or chili. Just some [2] _____ rice and chicken – and drink plenty of water.
2 What about today's special? It's really [3] _____ . Everybody loves it!
3 How would you like your fish, sir – [4] _____ over an open fire or [5] _____ in olive oil?
4 Can you cook this meat a little more? It's still [6] _____ .
5 Don't eat that yogurt! It smells very [7] _____ to me. I think it's bad.
6 We normally eat [8] _____ meat in my country. We cook it in the oven for a long time so it is very easy to eat.

## 8.1 TRAVELING (page 76)

A **Look at the words in the box. Find words that mean …**

| | | | | |
|---|---|---|---|---|
| airplane | backpack | bus station | check-in counter | guidebook |
| map | suitcase | tour bus | tour guide | tourists |

1 two places where you begin or end a trip: _____ _____

2 two objects that give you information about a city: _____

_____

3 people who are on vacation: _____

4 a person who takes you to interesting sights when you're on vacation: _____

5 two kinds of luggage: _____ _____

B **Use the correct form of the words in the box in exercise A to complete the sentences. Use each word or phrase only <u>one</u> time.**

1 Last time I went to the airport, it was awful. I arrived very late, and there was a long line at the _____ .

2 We live near the airport, so we often see _____ in the sky over our house.

3 When I go on vacation, I always take two big _____ . One for my clothes and one for the things I buy. My sister doesn't like shopping, so she just brings one large

_____ .

4 Last year I worked as a _____ . I worked on a _____ . It left from the central _____ and took people all around the city. The _____ loved it!

5 When I visit a new city, I always buy a local _____ to tell me about the best restaurants. Then I use the _____ on my phone to help me find them!

## 8.2 USING TRANSPORTATION (page 78)

A (Circle) **the correct verbs to complete the text.**

I usually go to work by bus. It takes me about 45 minutes. I leave home at 7:15. I walk two blocks to the bus stop and I ¹*get in / get on* the number 72 bus. The 72 takes me to the park. There, I ²*pick up / change* buses and take the 35. Sometimes I ³*miss / catch* the 35, and then I have to wait and ⁴*take / miss* the 44. The 35 ⁵*gets into / drops me off* right in front of my office. The 44 stops several long blocks away. If it's a nice day, it's OK. I can walk to work from there. If I'm late, I ⁶*get onto / get into* a taxi. I get to the office at 8 o'clock.

B **Choose the correct verbs from the box and write them in the correct form to complete the texts.**

| | |
|---|---|
| catch | change |
| drop off | get into |
| get off | get on |
| get out of | miss |
| pick up | take |

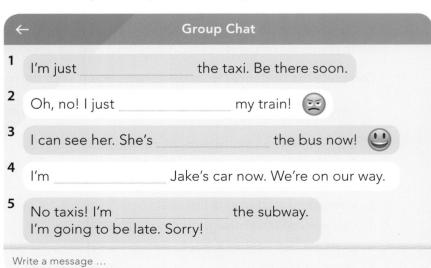

**Group Chat**

1 I'm just _____ the taxi. Be there soon.

2 Oh, no! I just _____ my train! 😠

3 I can see her. She's _____ the bus now! 😊

4 I'm _____ Jake's car now. We're on our way.

5 No taxis! I'm _____ the subway. I'm going to be late. Sorry!

Write a message …

## 9.1 NAMING ACCESSORIES (page 86)

**A** **Look at the pictures. Make sentences with *He's/She's (not) wearing* and the accessory words in the box.**

*He's wearing sunglasses.*

| | | | | |
|---|---|---|---|---|
| belt | bracelet | earring(s) | glove(s) | necklace |
| scarf | sneakers | sunglasses | tie | |

**B** (Circle) **the correct words to complete the sentences.**
1 I need a *belt / bracelet / tie*. My pants are too big.
2 My hands are cold. Where are my *gloves / sneakers / socks*?
3 You need a *bracelet / necklace / scarf* in this cold weather.
4 She's wearing *a scarf / sunglasses / a tie*, so I can't see her eyes.
5 I love your *earrings / gloves / socks*. Are they real gold?

## 9.2 DESCRIBING APPEARANCE (page 88)

**A** **Look at the words in the box. Choose the correct words to match the descriptions.**

| | | | | |
|---|---|---|---|---|
| bald | beard | curly | dark | gray |
| light | mustache | pierced ears | straight | |

1 the hair on your face: _____
2 what you have if you wear earrings: _____
3 a way to describe a head without hair on it: _____
4 ways to describe hair color: _____
5 ways to describe how hair looks: _____

**B** **Complete the sentences with words from exercise A. You won't need all of the words.**
1 Do most people in your family have dark or _____ hair?
2 I don't wear earrings because I don't have _____ .
3 Does he have a mustache and a _____ ?
4 My father is completely _____ , but all my brothers have a lot of hair.
5 Is her hair straight or _____ ?
6 One of my grandmothers has normal _____ hair, but my other grandmother colors her hair bright red!

## 10.1 DESCRIBING JOBS (page 98)

A **Circle** the best words to complete the sentences.

1 Wow! That's an amazing building. Who was the *photographer / architect*?
2 My sister is a *call center worker / nurse*. She spends all day on the phone.
3 I have a problem with my car. I need to call *an engineer / a mechanic*.
4 The *receptionist / police officer* recommended the hotel restaurant.
5 Lie down and relax. The *photographer / nurse* said you need to rest.
6 I asked a *call center worker / police officer* to help when somebody took my purse.

B **Match the jobs to the things people say.**

| accountant | dentist | IT specialist | lawyer |
|---|---|---|---|
| paramedic | physical therapist | project manager | |

1 _____

"My client, Mr. Gaston, did not steal the money."

2 _____

"Give all your receipts to me. I manage the business's money."

3 _____

"Sorry, but I think you have a software problem."

4 _____

"OK, now carefully stretch out your left leg. Good!"

5 _____

"The work has to be completed by April 10. We're on schedule."

6 _____

"Open your mouth wide, please."

7 _____

"Now we're going to take you to the hospital."

## 10.2 DESCRIBING HEALTH PROBLEMS (page 100)

A **Circle** the correct verbs to complete the phrases for injuries and illnesses.

1 *break / catch* a cold
2 *break / get* your leg
3 *catch / have* a sore throat
4 *catch / hurt* the flu
5 *cut / have* a stomachache
6 *cut / have* a toothache
7 *cut / have* your finger
8 *break / bang* your head
9 *feel / have* a fever
10 *hurt / cut* yourself shaving
11 *get / hurt* your back
12 *have / hurt* a headache
13 *catch / twist* your ankle

B **Complete the sentences using a phrase from exercise A. For some sentences, there is more than one possible answer. Make sure to use the right form of the verbs and pronouns that fit the sentences.**

1 Did you _____ in a skiing accident?
2 Don't _____ with that knife!
3 Go to the dentist if you _____ .
4 I _____ because I ate too much.
5 I _____ because of the loud music.
6 People often _____ when they have a cold or the flu.
7 You _____ . It's 39.4 degrees!
8 There was blood on his shirt because he _____ .

## 11.1 USING VERB-NOUN INTERNET PHRASES (page 108)

A **Match the ten phrases to the definitions.**

| | | |
|---|---|---|
| 1  add someone as a friend | 2  build a website | 3  change your password |
| 4  check your messages | 5  click on a link | 6  join a group |
| 7  make a video | 8  message someone | 9  open a social media account |
| 10  swipe left or right | | |

a   press the mouse on text to go to a website ___
b   move the screen to one side or the other ___
c   record and edit live action ___
d   see if you have any new email or texts ___
e   create your online identity ___

f   contact someone by electronic text ___
g   make a new internet destination ___
h   choose a different security code ___
i   include another person in your network ___
j   become a member ___

B (Circle) **the best phrases to complete the sentences.**
1   I never *check my messages / build websites* on a computer. I just use my phone.
2   In some apps, to show that you like something, you can *swipe right / message someone.*
3   Oh, no! I *clicked a link / joined a group,* and now my computer has a virus.
4   I like my boss, but I don't want to *add her as a friend / open an account for her* on social media.
5   At my office we have to *change our passwords / make videos* every six months. It's important to be safe.

## 11.2 USING SOCIAL MEDIA VERBS (page 111)

A **Replace the icon with a verb from the box. Which of these sentences are true for you? Tell a partner.**

| | | | | |
|---|---|---|---|---|
| download | go viral | like | search for | share |

1   I usually _____ 👍 photos of my friends.
2   I love to watch cat videos, and I _____ 🔗 them on social media with my friends.
3   I _____ ⬇ lots of videos, but I don't have time to see them all.
4   If some of my videos _____ ✳ , I'll be so happy! I want everyone to see my work.
5   I sometimes _____ 🔍 information about Australia. I really want to visit there someday.

B **Complete the sentences with the correct verb from the box. Are the sentences true for you? Change them if they are not.**

| | | | | |
|---|---|---|---|---|
| block | bookmark | follow | log in | upload |

1   To see "My Account" information on my bank's website, I have to _____ with my username and password.
2   I _____ people on social media if they post things I don't want to see.
3   I _____ lots of famous people on social media. I like to know what they're doing.
4   I have my own website, and I _____ my videos there so other people can enjoy them.
5   If I go online and find a site that I like, I always _____ it so I don't lose it.

## 12.1 DESCRIBING WEATHER (page 118)

A   **Look at the pictures. Which weather words from the box do you associate with the pictures?**

| | | | | |
|---|---|---|---|---|
| blizzard | boiling | cloudy | drought | flood |
| foggy | freezing | humid | hurricane | rainy |
| snowstorm | snowy | sunny | thunder and lightning | windy |

1   Picture A: _____
2   Picture B: _____
3   Picture C: _____
4   Picture D: _____
5   Picture E: _____

B   **Replace the weather symbols with the correct words.**

The weather today is warm and ¹_____ ⚡, with the maximum temperature of 23°C. But it's going to be ²_____ ☁ in the morning and ³_____ 🌧 in the afternoon. We might even get some ⁴_____ ⛈ in the evening, and it'll be very ⁵_____ 🌬 all day. If we get a lot of rain, we may have a ⁶_____ 🌊, so be extra careful if you're driving!

*Write a message …*

Brrr, it's ⁷_____ ❄ out there today, so wear your warmest clothes. Later on this evening, we can expect to get a ⁸_____ 🌩 that will last all night. Tomorrow will continue to be ⁹_____ 🌨, so stay home if you can.

*Write a message …*

## 12.2 DESCRIBING LANDSCAPES AND CITYSCAPES (page 120)

A   **Look at the map. Find <u>ten</u> of the features from the box on the map. Label them.**

1   cave
2   cliff
3   coast
4   fountain
5   glacier
6   rainforest
7   rocks
8   statue
9   tower
10   waterfall

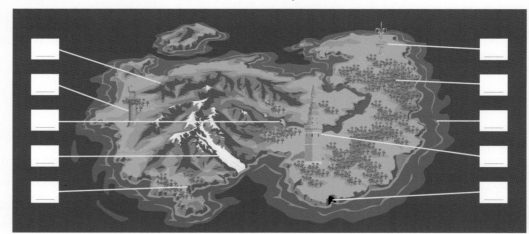

B   **Choose the best word to complete the texts.**

1   It's a beautiful place on the *coast / glacier*. There's a big wide beach at the foot of a tall *field / cliff*. There are some *valleys / caves* there also, so you can keep out of the sun when it's too hot.

2   Downtown there are some tall *skyscrapers / waterfalls* and a big open square with a *fountain / cave* in the middle. It's a great place to go in the evening to hang out with friends.

# PROGRESS CHECK

Can you do these things? Check (✓) what you can do. Then write your answers in your notebook.

| Now I can … | Prove it |
| --- | --- |
| ☐ use food words. | Write three count and five non-count food words. |
| ☐ talk about quantities. | Write about the quantities of different kinds of food you eat every week. Use *a little, a few, a lot of,* etc. |
| ☐ use adjectives to describe food. | Write five adjectives for preparing food and five adjectives for flavor. |
| ☐ talk about what I like to do. | Complete the sentences about food with a verb + *to* + verb, or a verb + verb + *-ing*.<br>*I would like … I enjoy …* |
| ☐ order food in a restaurant. | Write one expression a customer uses and one expression a server uses in a restaurant. |
| ☐ give my opinion in an online comment. | Look at your comment from lesson 7.4, exercise 2E. Can you make it better? Find three ways. |

| Now I can … | Prove it |
| --- | --- |
| ☐ use words to talk about traveling | Write two kinds of luggage, two places you travel from, and six other vacation words. |
| ☐ talk about travel and vacation preferences. | Complete these sentences: *When I'm on vacation, I usually …*<br>*If I can, I always …* |
| ☐ use verbs to talk about transportation and trips. | Write five verbs you can use with *bus* or *train*. |
| ☐ talk about reasons. | Write three reasons why you're learning English. Use *to* or *for*. |
| ☐ make suggestions and give advice. | Write two ways to suggest a plan for this evening. |
| ☐ give advice in a short comment. | Look at your comment from lesson 8.4, exercise 3D. Can you make it better? Find three ways. |

| Now I can … | Prove it |
| --- | --- |
| ☐ use words for fashion accessories. | Write two accessories you wear on your feet, two accessories you wear around your neck, and five other accessories. |
| ☐ compare two things, people, or places. | Write sentences to compare these two pairs of things: sneakers/socks  New York/my hometown |
| ☐ use words to describe a person's face and hair. | Write two words for hair on the face and three words to describe hair. |
| ☐ compare two or more different things, people, or places. | Complete this sentence: *The _____ (good) place to take pictures in my city is …* |
| ☐ ask for and give opinions. | Write one way of asking for an opinion and one way of giving an opinion. |
| ☐ write a paragraph about an image. | Look at your paragraph from lesson 9.4, exercise 2D. Can you make it better? Find three ways. |

# PROGRESS CHECK

**Can you do these things? Check (✓) what you can do. Then write your answers in your notebook.**

| Now I can … | Prove it |
|---|---|
| ☐ use words for jobs. | Write two dangerous jobs, two office jobs, and four other jobs. |
| ☐ talk about things that are necessary. | Write one thing you have to do and one thing you don't have to do in this class. |
| ☐ use words for health problems. | Write two phrases for different accidents, two ways you feel when you get sick, and two other health problems. |
| ☐ make predictions | Complete these predictions:<br>*One day I'll … I probably won't … Next year I might …* |
| ☐ ask for and offer help. | Write three different ways of asking about a problem. |
| ☐ write an email giving advice. | Look at your email from lesson 10.4, exercise 2C. Can you make it better? Find three ways. |

| Now I can … | Prove it |
|---|---|
| ☐ use phrases to talk about the internet | Write six phrases for things you can do on the internet. |
| ☐ talk about experiences | Write about an experience you've had and one you haven't had. |
| ☐ use verbs to talk about social media | Write three verbs you can use with *videos* and two verbs you can use with *people*. |
| ☐ talk about experiences and give more information. | Write about something exciting you've done. When did you do it? |
| ☐ make and respond to requests. | Write one way to make a request and one way to respond to a request. |
| ☐ write a comment about an infographic. | Look at your comment from lesson 11.4, exercise 2D. Can you make it better? Find three ways. |

| Now I can … | Prove it |
|---|---|
| ☐ use words to describe weather | Write three words to describe hot weather, three words to describe cold weather, and three words to describe wet weather. |
| ☐ ask questions with *be like*. | Complete the sentences: *What _____ the festival last week? What _____ the weather _____ tomorrow?* |
| ☐ use words to describe landscapes | Write two words to describe the landscape near your home, two landscape features that you can't find near your town, and two other landscape features you like. |
| ☐ use *who*, *which*, and *that* to give more information about people and objects. | Complete these sentences: *She's the woman who … That's the picture which … This is the beach that …* |
| ☐ ask for and give directions. | Write two different ways to ask for directions. Write three different ways to give directions. |
| ☐ write a simple set of instructions. | Look at your instructions from lesson 12.4, exercise 3D. Can you make them better? Find three ways. |

This page is intentionally left blank

# PAIR WORK PRACTICE

## 7.3  EXERCISE 2D  STUDENT A

**Situation 1**

Imagine you're in a restaurant. Ask the waiter what he recommends. You're a pescetarian (you eat fish but not meat). Use *I mean* to be clear about what you eat and what you don't eat.

**Situation 2**

Imagine you're a waiter in a restaurant. Ask if the customer would like dessert. Recommend the strawberry cheesecake. Now recommend the fruit salad. Yes, there are a few strawberries in the fruit salad.

## 8.3  EXERCISE 2C  STUDENT A

1  **Ask student B for some suggestions for what to do when you have free time in a city. Listen and respond. Use an echo question if necessary.**

2  **Give student B some advice using the suggestions below:**

Go to the mall with a group of friends. It's only half an hour by car.

Have something to eat at a local café (please use the name of a real local café). It's pretty cheap and has good food.

Go to the movies. There's a great movie playing now that won an Academy Award, and it starts at 8:30 p.m.

## 11.3  EXERCISE 2D  STUDENT A

1  **Complete the sentences with a question from the Real-world strategy box. Then ask your partner.**

   1  When your phone has no power. _____ it?

   2  Those black and white pictures on the page. You use your phone to read them. What _____ ?

   3  The person who invented cell phones. What _____ ?

2  **Now listen to your partner. Answer their questions with one of these answers:**

   It's called "**international roaming**."     They're called **SIM cards**.     You **upload** it.

This page is intentionally left blank

# PAIR WORK PRACTICE

## 7.3 EXERCISE 2D    STUDENT B

**Situation 1**

Imagine you're a waiter in a restaurant. Ask if the customer would like to order now. Recommend the chicken. Then recommend the beef.

**Situation 2**

Imagine you're in a restaurant and you would like to order dessert. Ask the waiter what he recommends. You're allergic to strawberries (you can't eat any strawberries). Use *I mean* to be clear about what you can and can't eat.

## 8.3 EXERCISE 2C    STUDENT B

1   **Give student A some advice using the suggestions or ideas of your own.**

Visit the local museum. It's only $5.00 per person and has a really interesting section on local history.

Go shopping for souvenirs. Stores open at 9:30 a.m., and there's a sale.

Rent a bike. It's a really cheap way to see the city, and there's a docking station a block from your hotel.

2   **Ask student A for some suggestions for what to do after class today. Listen and respond. Use an echo question if necessary.**

## 11.3 EXERCISE 2D    STUDENT B

1   **Listen to your partner. Answer his/her questions with one of these answers:**

His name is Martin Cooper.        They're **QR codes**.        You say "my phone's dead."

2   **Now complete the sentences with a question from the Real-world strategy box. Then ask your partner.**

   **1**   When you want to put a photo on a social media site. What _____ ?

   **2**   Those things in your phone that hold data. What _____ ?

   **3**   When you use your phone in another country. _____ it?